Praise for *Th*
and l

"*The Architecture of Grammar* is an expertly written masterclass on how to use grammar to write successfully. You may be learning English as a second language or brushing up on your grammar skills to become an author. Whatever your writing goal is, this book is your perfect resource to help you get a great start and accomplish it with excellence."

—David Diehl, D.Ed.

"Léandre takes complex concepts and presents them in such a way that anyone can understand them. He's managed to quickly teach me everything that I wish my teachers in high school and college could have in an easy, digestible format. [Léandre] will help you untie the knots that are preventing you from experiencing your full potential as a writer. With his guidance, you will gain an immense amount of confidence to begin writing your own story that will undoubtedly impact everyone around you."

—Alelia Thompson, MBA.

"If you want to write proficiently, I really recommend Léandre. You probably already write, but he will help you understand the different types of writing. He'll help you improve the engagement with your audience. If you are thinking of writing a book, writing for social media, or just writing for your business, then I definitely recommend checking out what Léandre does."

—Angela Reid, GDiLT

THE ARCHITECTURE OF GRAMMAR

30 SHORT LESSONS TO THINK ABOUT A PENTHOUSE AND IMPROVE YOUR WRITING THROUGH GRAMMAR

LÉANDRE LAROUCHE

ABOUT THE AUTHOR

Léandre Larouche is an author, speaker, and writing consultant based in Toronto, Canada. He is the author of *Hétérochrome* (2017), *Write a Book That Matters* (2021), and *The End of Nonsense* (forthcoming). Though he grew up in French in Saguenay, Québec, Léandre has been writing in English for the better part of the last decade. He studied English literature and professional writing at Concordia University, where he also worked as a writing assistant and developed a unique writing methodology. Léandre Larouche was a 2019-2020 Fulbright fellow at Lycoming College in Williamsport, PA. Upon coming back to Canada during the COVID-19 pandemic, he founded Trivium Writing Inc.

For Rose and the

Green Valley College team

Trivium Empire Press
Toronto, Ont., Canada
triviumempirepress.com

ISBN 978-1-7777822-2-1

Credits
Cover page photo: Chris Barbalis
Set in Baskerville
Design: PMW.net
Review and correction by Aris Kalamaras

TRIVIUM EMPIRE PRESS

Table of Contents

FOREWORD

By Judy Cuggy Lapalme

I first met Léandre as a professor in the Composition and Professional Writing program at Concordia University in Montreal. It was during the first class where I usually present the syllabus, the class rules, and the goals and outcomes for the class. An easy class, a short class usually, and we are off and away quickly after the presentations. A student stayed after (there is always one!), and it was Léandre, a bright-looking young man, who came to discuss the course and the coursework.

During our conversation, Léandre made clear he wanted to know how this course would fit in with his plans. He was also concerned about being away attending a Fulbright Canada program later that September. At a university where many students worked full-time or part-time, I was always happy to accommodate students who were managing complicated schedules.

I was more than happy to be flexible with Léandre, who was participating in a think tank of young people from across North America. I told him that this was fine with me as long as he was willing to share his experience with his classmates. Léandre was very happy to do so. I was impressed to see how well he presented in English even though this was clearly not his first language.

During one of our many meetings, I asked Léandre why he, a French speaker, chose a degree in English Literature when he came from a town so far from Montreal with no exposure to English. Not only would he have to speak English, but he would also have to understand the literature deeply and then write about it meaningfully and convincingly to manage his assignments. He wanted the challenge, he said. He was determined to learn and devote himself to mastering his English and especially his writing.

Over the years that I have taught Léandre, I have come to know an individual who continually challenges himself to achieve in the classroom and at the university. I have followed Léandre's growth at Concordia and witnessed his drive to learn and experience everything that his university could offer him. He participated in exchange programs, volunteered in student organizations, entered writing competitions, became a writing tutor, all while working hard in his courses.

I have been a member of the English department faculty at Concordia University since 2005 on a part-time and full-time basis and. At one point, I was the Coordinator of the Professional Writing and Composition program. I have also worked as a professional writer in various sectors, bringing me real experience in the value of writing.

As a professor, I am very much invested in impressing students with the power and importance of writing—how writing well immediately provides the writer with a voice and an audience and how making certain mistakes can remove that audience very quickly. An inadvertent spelling or grammar error or inconsistent tone can lead the reader to reject the content outright, almost unconsciously.

What does it mean to write well? A starting point is knowing what you want to say and then building the framework to communicate your ideas. The building blocks include grammar, purpose, audience, and style. Finding a suitable textbook that is comprehensive, but not overly lengthy and intimidating, has been a daunting task.

As I read Léandre's book, it is very clear that he shares the same vision about the power of writing. He brings the good news that it does not have to be so very difficult. Who better to write about how to write powerfully in English than one who has walked the walk and learned from everyone he met? Léandre has used his own experience as a student of English and as a coach for students wanting to learn English to simplify and declutter the perceived complexity of writing well. In *The Architecture of Grammar*, Léandre breaks down grammar and writing into manageable chunks to encourage his readers to move forward confidently. Léandre is an engaging writer and individual, and his readers will enjoy and benefit from his light-hearted approach to an often-intimidating topic.

INTRODUCTION

Grammar is a real-world skill because writing well opens a world of new, exciting opportunities. What makes it difficult isn't writing itself; it is the way writing is taught.

English grammar is hard for most people. For native English speakers, it's difficult to make sense of all the rules, while for non-native English speakers, the exceptions are too confusing. Although grammar is a great tool for success, we often see it as boring, tedious, and unnecessary.

There are two reasons we feel that grammar is hard and unimportant. First, most modern societies no longer value writing as a critical life skill. Second, we often learn grammar without applying it to something we love. This is a huge problem. Writing is one of the most powerful skills in the world, and we can learn grammar while exploring topics we love.

Grammar is a real-world skill because writing well opens a world of new, exciting opportunities. What makes it difficult isn't the act of writing; it is the way writing is taught.

I was an unlikely candidate to master English grammar. I grew up in a small town in Canada where no one spoke the language. I was raised speaking French, and it wasn't until I was about twelve years old that I started studying English.

When I decided to become a writer at 15 years old, I wanted more. I began writing in French because it was my mother tongue, but I had my eyes on a bigger prize: the English-speaking market. In truth, I felt limited by my hometown, and I wanted to live in the large North American cities where people speak English. Growing up in Québec, learning how to speak and write fluently in English was my little American Dream.

Ten years later, as I write this introduction in my apartment in the city of Toronto, Ontario, I can't help looking at the journey without a deep sense of satisfaction. The journey to English mastery wasn't easy, but it's been well worth it. Today I see it has given my life meaning and brought me the success I enjoy. I wouldn't be where I am if it hadn't been for writing.

I can attribute my successful life to writing for two reasons. First, I made writing my obsession; I studied like a mad scientist. Picking a skill or a field and working hard to master is hard work, and one of the surest ways to live a fulfilling life. Second, writing is an amplifier. By its very nature, it has the capacity to make us more successful and help us realize our dreams. It is, in fact, one of the most powerful skills in the world.

The power of writing can't be overstated. We live in an information era when more content than ever is published. The more content is published, the more easily we get bored. Yet if we wish our ideas to be heard and understood, we must write. We must write eloquently, too. We must grab and sustain our readers' attention.

The beautiful thing about writing is that the eloquence we develop by doing it isn't limited to writing. Our ability to write well shows in the way we speak, think, and make decisions. Writing is simply formalized thinking. If we can put together a compelling text, we can speak compellingly, too (with practice). Our thinking also becomes more structured, more deliberate, and more mindful.

Although we never admit this publicly, we judge people harshly based on their writing. We don't necessarily realize it, but we do. Unconsciously, we associate a person's ability to express a sentence clearly and professionally to their status and intelligence. This is not a conscious thought process, but we can't help making those judgments. If we want the best chance to live a successful life, we must take writing seriously.

Grammar is a critical part of writing because it holds ideas together for us to understand them. Three elements make or break writing: grammar, logic, and rhetoric. Together, these elements are known as the "Trivium," and they are the first pillars of a person's education. While logic (the art of thinking) and rhetoric (the art of convincing) matter, they mean little with poor grammar.

Grammar is the code through which we humans communicate. Every language has its grammar, and through grammar we decipher what words mean. We can use words all we want, but if we don't use them with proper grammar, our audience won't understand what we mean. Some grammar mistakes are of little consequence. At worst, they make us look unprofessional. But some grammar mistakes hinder our message and make our ideas incomprehensible.

Grammar is as much a code as mathematics. It's made of pieces we must place in the right order. To understand these pieces, we must learn certain concepts, and we need to do so in the right sequence. For most people, the concepts that explain the pieces of grammar are too abstract and obscure. We can't blame anyone for that: Most writing instruction lacks clarity and passion.

This book, however, is going to change the way you look at grammar. It will teach you the grammar foundations you need to write clearly and professionally without wasting time on useless details. You can be a beginner or an expert writer and benefit from this book. The goal for this book is not only to teach you the concepts, but also to give you the opportunity to use them in a way that's interesting to you.

I promise to make this book as interesting and relevant to you as possible. But to do so, I need your help. I need you to think of the biggest dream you currently have. Look at your bucket list and pick the one thing that excites you the most. The dream should be an action that you can make. Think about yourself making this action in the third person. For example, mine could be, "Léandre buys a penthouse in New York City." I'll actually be using different versions of this sentence throughout this book.

Whatever your dream is, stick to it while you read this book. You will be applying the grammar lessons to your dream. This book includes thirty grammar rules you should know. Each lesson includes examples and exercises. Because the grammar rules require using different words and sentence structures, you will write multiple sentences about your dream.

As you write sentences to learn grammar rules, you will develop a short story about your dream. By the time you are done reading this book, you will have a short text. This short text will be a representation of your biggest dream. You will be able to use this text to complete exercises at the end of the book. More importantly, you will have written about something you love.

I chose to teach you grammar through your dream because grammar has helped me realize mine. I am a strong believer in the power of writing, and I will do everything I can to convince you of how important it is. But I cannot simply convince you it is important. I must give you a reason to care, and I am giving you on now: Grammar will make your wildest dreams come true.

It starts now.

Part 1

The Basics

Lesson 1

We Build Sentences by Stacking Information Blocks on Top of One Another

Writing is always answering questions—even if no question was asked. Everything we see in writing could be turned into a question. The information blocks we are dealing with are question words.

Your dream has several layers of depth which you can explore.

Whoever has told you that grammar is complicated was lying. Grammar is simple. There is one main concept you must understand, which is that sentences are made of **information blocks**. Once you understand this, learning and understanding grammar becomes easy. Rules and exceptions describe the relationship between information blocks in a sentence.

In this lesson, you will

- Learn what the components of a sentence are
- Understand how information blocks build sentences
- Discover the pyramid of sentence structure

Components of a Sentence

These are the different components of a sentence:

- **Parts of speech** are different *word categories* that give us isolated pieces of information such as "who," "what," "where," "which," "whose," "when," "how," and "why." Every word in a sentence is a part of speech.

In *"Léandre bought the penthouse,"* there are four words, which means there are four parts of speech.

- **Word Roles** express *the role* a word plays in a sentence. Unlike parts of speech, word roles don't say what words are; they say what words do.

In *"Léandre bought the penthouse," "Léandre"* plays one role, *"buy"* plays another, and *"the penthouse"* another.

- **Phrases** are groups of words that convey more complete information such as "who," "what," "where," "which," "whose," "when," "to whom," "how," and "why."

*"**In** New York City"* is a prepositional phrase that indicates the WHEN in a sentence.

- **Clauses:** Clauses are *simple ideas*, or incomplete thoughts, that do not allow you to convey an understandable point. They allow you to express part of a point.

*"**After** Léandre bought the penthouse"* is a dependent clause because it has a coordination conjunction.

- **Sentences:** Sentences are *complex ideas*, or thoughts, that allow you to convey an understandable point. They're made of one or multiple clauses, phrases, word roles, and parts of speech.

In the sentence, "After he bought the penthouse, Léandre went to get a drink," there are two clauses, four phrases, four word roles, and eleven parts of speech.

Here is another example:

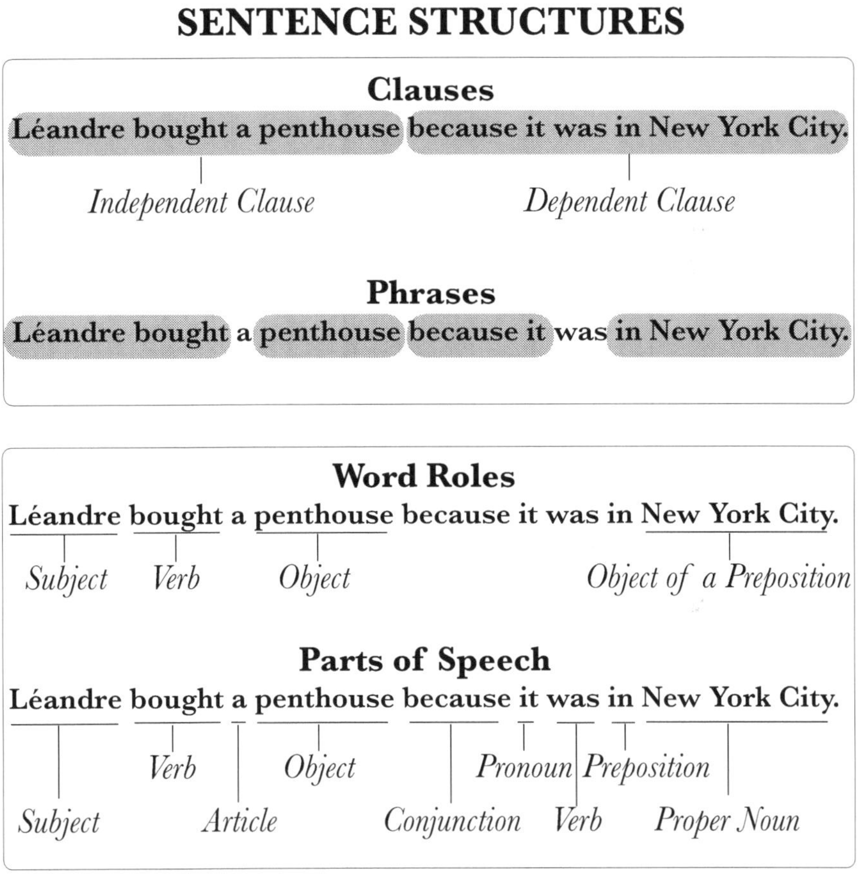

Graphic 1. The Anatomy of a Sentence

Information Blocks and Question Words

Writing works like architecture. We build texts by putting blocks together. But what are these blocks made of? **Information blocks** are made of answers to questions. Every part of a text serves to answer questions. As a result, we can also think of **information blocks** as question words.

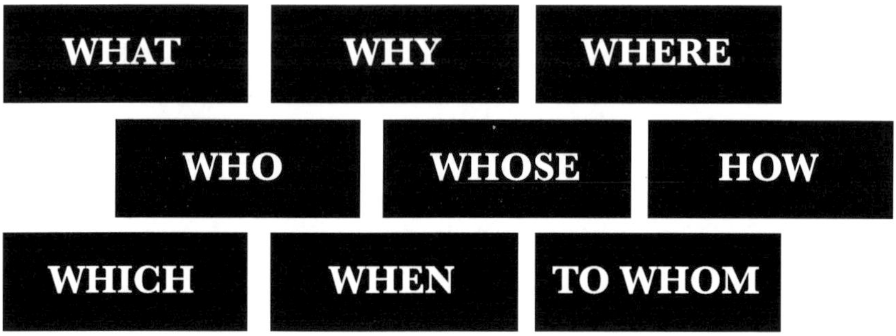

Graphic 1. Questions Words

- WHO: Léandre
- WHAT: bought a penthouse
- WHY: because it was in New York City

The **question words** above represent the information you provide while writing. You can use these **question words** at different **textual levels**. A sentence includes 4 levels

The Pyramid of Writing

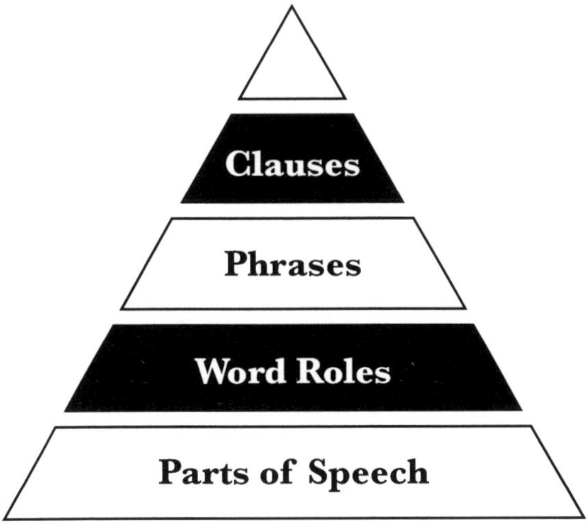

Graphic 2. The Sentence Pyramid

The pyramid above shows you the interior of a sentence. In order of complexity, a sentence is made of *clauses, phrases, word roles, and parts of speech*. You need **parts of speech** to make word roles, **word roles** to make phrases, **phrases** to make clauses, and clauses to make sentences. Writing works exactly like architecture.

In the sentence, *"After he bought the penthouse, Léandre went to get a drink,"* the eleven parts of speech turn into four word roles, four of which turn into four phrases, and together create two clauses, which makes a sentence.

Congratulations! You've just learned the most important grammar concept. This lesson covered the components of a sentence, how information blocks build sentences, and the pyramid of sentence structure. Now, you may not understand every concept at a technical level yet, but you now understand the architecture of a sentence. In the next lesson, you will learn how to make sure your sentence is always grammatically correct.

Lesson 2

Sentences Must Include Someone Doing Something

Like in a story, you need a character and an action to create an English sentence.

If your dream lacks a character or an action, your dream dies.

English is a straightforward language. Without someone doing something, you have no sentence. Imagine this: I tell you a story, but I only tell you about the characters, not what they do. Would you understand? Exactly. What if I told you about the actions in the story and nothing of the characters who perform them? Would you understand the story? Right.

In this lesson, you will

- Learn that sentences are like stories
- Understand how word roles drive the story of a sentence
- Explore different word roles (subject, verb, direct object)
- Understand which parts of speech go into which word roles

Sentences are Like Stories

Like in a story, you need a character and an action to create an English sentence. In most cases, you also need a receiver of the action, but we'll talk more about that later. For now, just remember that the **subject**, the **verb**, and the **direct object** are the most important word roles.

(Subject)	(Verb)	(Direct Object)
Ex. Léandre	bought	the penthouse.
WHO	**WHAT**	

Remember the **question words**? As far as question words go, you need a WHO and a WHAT in a sentence. These are the two basic pieces of information you need. Someone must be doing something. If no one is doing anything, you have no sentence.

Word Roles Drive the Story of a Sentence

Before we go any further, I want to remind you of the dream you picked while reading the introduction. The upcoming lessons are based on this dream, and you are going to use it many times as you go through this book.

Understand that, without at least a **subject** and a **verb** in your sentence, you must say goodbye to your dream. If you forget the **subject**, you disappear from your biggest dream. You forget the **verb** and the dream dies unaccomplished before you. This is dramatic, but that's how important it is to have someone doing something in an English sentence.

It's the difference between achieving your dream and not achieving it.

No matter what you do, remember that you need a **subject** and a **verb**—a character and an action. You need yourself and the action you want to perform—the WHO and the WHAT. Nothing else matters if you miss these two elements. After all, you can't build without a foundation. If this happens, you need to go back and ask yourself, "who is doing what in this sentence?" You need to ask yourself, "who is the character and what action is he doing?"

Your Commitment

Below I want you to write your dream (e.g., "Léandre buys a penthouse.") and I want you to sign your name, affirming you will always have a **subject** and a **verb** in your sentences.

Your Sentence

____

____

Your Signature

____

By now, you know the main word roles that go into a sentence—subjects, verbs, and direct objects. But word roles only tell you what role a word plays; they don't tell you what category of word it is. It's important to differentiate the different types of words because they are used in different ways. The types of words are known as **parts of speech**. There are many parts of speech, but we'll only focus on the ones necessary for the WHO and the WHAT.

Subjects Are Made of Nouns

The subject of your sentence must be the character of the story your sentence is telling. For example, in "Léandre will buy a penthouse," "Léandre" is the subject. We use nouns to identify people, animals, plants, objects, places, etc. There exists different types of nouns, which creates a variety of possible sentence subjects.

Noun type	Definition	Examples
Common nouns	refer to people or things **in genera**l.	man, woman, police-man, teenager, city, park, etc.
Proper nouns	identify a **particular** person, place or thing	Toronto, Canada, Justin Trudeau, Friday, etc.
Abstract nouns	refer to **intangible** ideas, qualities, and conditions.	truth, danger, expe-rience, compatibility, etc.
Collective nouns	refer to **groups** of people or things.	audience, family, government, team, group, jury, etc.
Count nouns	refer to nouns that **can be counted** and thus have a plural form.	books, shelves, tables, apples, etc.
Mass nouns	refer to nouns that **cannot be counted** and so don't have a plural form. They are not preceded by an article (a, an, the	rain, flour, earth, wine, etc.

Determiners for Nouns

To understand nouns, we must understand determiners. **Determiners** clarify nouns. There are different determiners, and they clarify several things about the noun: they clarify whether its singular or plural, if it's specific or general, whom it belongs to, and its position. Sometimes, the number we need to express about a noun is not a number but a position. The position consists of the noun's number relative to other nouns.

Determiner type	Definition	Examples
Articles	express the **specificity** or **generality** of the noun	a, an, the, etc.
Demonstratives	express **the specificity or generality** of the noun.	this, that, these, those, which etc.
Possessive adjectives	indicate **to whom** an object belongs.	my, your, his, her, our, your (plural), their
Cardinal numbers	indicate **the specific amount** of people or objects	one, two, three, twenty, forty, etc
Ordinal numbers	indicate the **numeral position** of someone or something.	first, second, 1st 2nd, 3rd, first, next, last, etc.

Sometimes, the number we need to express about a noun is not a number but a position. The position consists of the noun's number relative to other nouns.

Pronouns Replace Nouns

Many times, we need to replace the noun with something else because we don't want to repeat it. We use pronouns to refer to nouns we've previously mentioned without being repetitive. There are different pronouns, which all represent different things.

Pronoun type	Definition	Example
Personal Pronouns	represent a **grammatical person**	he, she, they, it, etc.
Demonstrative pronouns	represent **nouns and their positions**	this, that, these, those, etc.
Interrogative pronouns (question words)	help formulate **questions**	which, who, what, where, etc.
Indefinite pronouns	represent people **without saying** exactly who they are	none, several, all, few, anything, etc.
Possessive pronouns	show something that **belongs** to someone	mine, yours, his, her, ours, yours, theirs

Verbs are Both a Word Role and a Part of Speech

Verbs are words that describe an action or indicate the existence of something. Depending on its type, a verb either shows what a noun is doing, what a noun is, or adds details to a noun.

Verb type	Definition	Examples
Action verbs	**express what happens** in a sentence.	see transitive and intransitive verbs below
Transitive verbs (action verb)	require a **direct object** to make sense.	bring, give, order, play, etc.
Intransitive verbs (action verb)	require **no direct object** to make sense.	adapt, fly, rise, shine, die, etc.
Linking verbs	**create a connection between** the subject and information about the subject.	act, appear, be, feel, remain, turn, etc.
Helping verbs	are placed **before another verb** to add detail.	can, may, must, shall, will, could, etc.

Direct Objects Are Made of Nouns Too

Like the subject, the **direct object** must be a **noun**. In the sentence, "Léandre will buy a penthouse," "a penthouse" is the direct object. In this case, the **noun** is accompanied by "a," a determiner. Most of the time, both your WHO and your WHAT are nouns. Remember that sentences are like stories, and we use **nouns** to identify people, animals, plants, objects, places, etc. Nouns identify the things that drive stories, which is why they are so important for sentences.

In this lesson, you've learned that sentences are like stories and explored the word roles and parts of speech that create sentences. You've also learned that a sentence always requires at minimum a WHO and a WHAT. In other words, you've learned the two most important **information blocks.** In the next lesson, you'll learn the order in which information blocks must come.

Lesson 3

Sentences Show Information Blocks in Order of Relevance

The first information block should be the most important and the last block the least important. As a writer, it is your job to place the information blocks in the right order. If you don't, your sentences won't make sense to your readers.

There is a sequence to your dream, and you must respect the sequence for your dream to occur.

The beauty of the English language is that it's both rich and simple. So far, by exploring the WHO and the WHAT of a sentence, we've only scratched the surface of sentences. We've only told one part of the story. The rest of the story lies in the context that comes with the WHO and the WHAT. To fully understand a story, we need context. We need to know not only WHO did WHAT, but WHEN, WHERE, HOW, and WHY.

In this lesson, you will

- Understand the difference between the active and the passive voice
- Learn that adjectives qualify nouns to add meaning
- Learn that adverbs qualify verbs to add details to actions
- Learn that prepositions link words together
- Discover the writing wall
- See emphasis in action
- Understand the problem of adding and removing blocks

The Difference Between Active and Passive Voice

We now know that WHO and WHAT are the most important information blocks in a sentence. But in which order should they come? Typically, WHO comes first. That's what we refer as "active voice." It means that "someone does something." The **active voice** is the most common form of writing because it's clear and engaging.

Active Voice (most common)

(Subject)	(Verb)	(Direct Object)
Léandre	buys	a penthouse.
WHO	WHAT	

Graphic 4. Active Voice

Passive voice, on the other hand, refers to "something done by someone." It places the emphasis on the object, not the subject. As a result, it makes our writing heavier and more difficult to understand. Passive voice is not very common and should be used only when necessary.

Passive Voice (only to hide the subject)

A penthouse is bought by Léandre

WHAT	WHO

Graphic 5. Passive Voice

It is only appropriate to use passive voice when:

- the direct object is more significant than the subject
- the subject is unknown and/or vague (Ex.: The crime was committed by a young man.)

Adjectives Qualify Nouns to Add Meaning

We use **adjectives** to modify a noun or a pronoun. We can place the adjective before the noun (ex. "an **old** man") or after if we also use a verb (Ex.: "The man is **old**").

Adjective type	Definition	Examples
Quantitative adjectives	express the **number** of the object discussed	See below.
(Quantitative) Definite numerals	give a **specific idea** of the number of nouns	See below.
Cardinals	**regular numbers**	one, two, three, four, five, six, etc.
Ordinals	tell us the position of a noun	first, second, third, fourth, fifth, etc.
Multiplicatives	Tell us how **many times** to multiply	single, double, tripe, quadruple
Indefinite numerals	Give a **vague idea** of the number of nouns	Few, all, many, several, etc.
Proper adjectives	Based **on names** and describe people, and things. They need to be capitalized	Russian, British, Canadian, American, Shakespearian, Renaissance, etc.
Descriptive, qualitative or attributive adjectives	Express **the nature** of the person or object discussed.	adaptable, brave, blue, dangerous, old, young, etc

Note that if you are listing several adjectives, you must respect the following order:

- Quantity or number
- Quality or opinion
- Size
- Age
- Shape
- Color
- Proper adjective (often nationality, other place of origin, or material)
- Purpose or qualifier

Ex.: Léandre bought two ***beautiful, 3,000-square-foot, rectangular*** *penthouses in New York City.*

Your Sentence

___

___

Ex.: Léandre bought two ***beautiful, grey, New York City*** *penthouses.*

Your Sentence

___

___

Ex.: Léandre bought two **beautiful, grey, vacation** *penthouses.*

Your Sentence

___

___

Adverbs Qualify Verbs

We use **adverbs** to modify a verb, an adjective, or another adverb. Adverbs can go either before or after the verb in a sentence, but the location of the adverb often changes the meaning of the phrase. (We will talk more about this in later lessons.)

Adverb type	Definition	Examples
Adverbs of time	help express the WHEN	already, today, tomorrow, now, then, yet, already, etc.
Adverbs of manner	help express the HOW	accidentally, badly, cruelly, kindly, poorly, etc.
Adverbs of degree	help express the to WHAT degree or to WHAT amount	almost, barely, extremely, just, nearly, very, deeply, etc.
Adverbs of place	help express the WHERE	above, abroad, back, behind, downstairs, here, etc.
Adverbs of frequency	help express the HOW OFTEN	always, constantly, daily, sometimes, etc.

Prepositions Link Words Together

We use **prepositions** to show the relationship between parts of speeches and phrases. Prepositions are tools that create meanings between other pieces of information.

Preposition type	Definition	Examples
Prepositions of time	help express the WHEN	**in** (April, the summer), **on** (Tuesday, Christmas day), **at** (noon, midnight), etc.
Prepositions of place	help express the WHERE	**at** (my house, the restaurant), **on** (the table), **in** (the city), etc.
Prepositions of direction or movement	help express the WHERE	**towards** (the bus stop), **to** (the shop), **through** (the glass), **into** (the ground), **to**, **from**, **under**, **along**, etc.
Prepositions of agent	help express the WHAT.	**by** (the judge), **with** (a pen), etc.
Prepositions of instrument	help express the HOW	**by** (plane), **with** (your key), **on** (my laptop), etc.

Conjunctions Link Phrases and Clauses

We use **conjunctions** to link phrases and clauses. Like prepositions, they help us create meaning between pieces of information. We will cover phrases in the next section of this lesson and clauses in the next lesson.

Conjunction type	Definition	Examples
Coordinating conjunctions	join **words, phrases, and clauses** together that are grammatically equal.	for, and, nor, but, or, yet, so (together, they are the FANBOYS)
Subordinating conjunction	introduce **dependent clauses** in a sentence and describe the relationship between clauses.	after, although, as far as, in that, once, since, supposing that, unless, when, etc.
Correlative conjunctions	join **equal sentence** elements to describe their relationship.	either… or; neither… nor; both… and; not only… but also.

The Writing Wall

With all these possible information blocks we can use, it's easy to feel confused. But the beauty of the English language is that it's very straightforward. We read sentences assuming that information blocks are presented in order of relevance. The first information block should be the most important and the last block the least important. As a writer, it is your job to place the information blocks in the right order. If you don't, your sentences won't make sense to your readers.

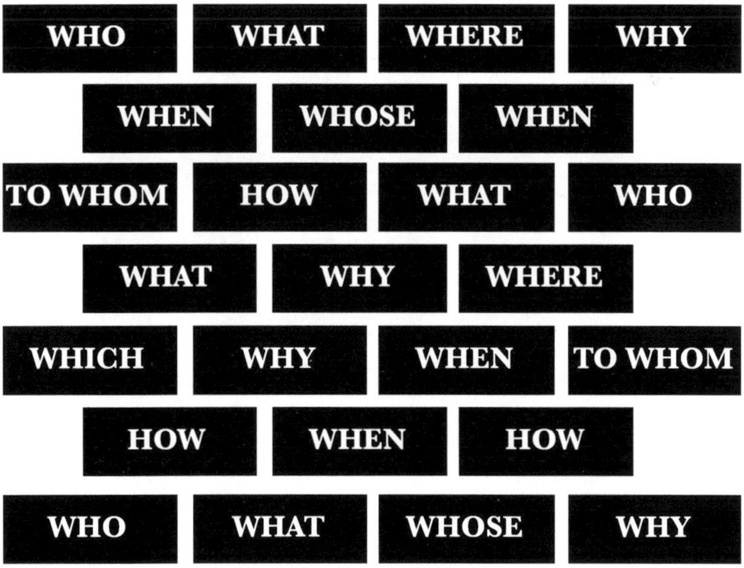

Graphic 6. The Writing Wall

You should read the writing wall like a text, which means from left to right. You can see it starts with WHO and WHAT and moves on to other information blocks such WHERE, WHY, WHEN, etc. Again, you must understand that the information blocks come in order of relevance. In other words, the closer an information block is to the beginning of a sentence, the more emphasis we place on it.

Note all the different types of emphasis you can use and write a sentence about your dream using each type of emphasis.

Emphasis in Action

Emphasis on WHO and WHAT

Ex.: ***Léandre will buy a penthouse*** *in New York City in 10 years because he likes the view.*

WHO **WHAT** **WHERE**

WHEN **WHY**

Your Sentence

Emphasis on WHERE

Ex.: ***In New York City****, Léandre will buy a penthouse because he likes the view.*

WHERE **WHO**

WHAT **WHY**

Your Sentence

Emphasis on WHY

*Ex.: **Because he likes the view**, Léandre will buy a penthouse in New York City in 10 years.*

WHY **WHO** **WHAT**

WHERE **WHEN**

Your Sentence

Emphasis on HOW

*Ex.: **Through a real estate agent**, Léandre will buy a penthouse in New York City in 10 years.*

HOW **WHO** **WHAT**

WHERE **WHEN**

Your Sentence

Emphasis on WHEN

Ex.: ***In 10 years**, Léandre will buy a penthouse in New York City because he likes the view.*

WHEN **WHO** **WHAT**

WHERE **WHY**

Your Sentence

What you notice from the last sentences is that you can add and remove information blocks as you wish. You can move the information blocks around, and by moving them around, you change the meaning of the sentence. Emphasis is meaning. What you focus on is a statement.

Problem of Adding and Removing Information Blocks

Even though information blocks come in order of importance, you still need to use your writer's judgment to decide how to structure a sentence. You will sometimes be called to change the structure a little bit because it either does not make a lot of sense or because it does not sound right. The more you add information blocks to a sentence, the more likely you are to run into those situations. You've likely noticed that I removed information blocks from the last few sentences. It does not make sense, for example, to write the following sentence:

Emphasis on HOW

Ex.: ***Through a real estate agent****, Léandre will buy a penthouse in New York City because he likes the view.*

HOW **WHO** **WHAT**

WHERE **WHY**

Your Sentence

The above sentence does not make sense because the HOW and the WHY are not related. Remember that information blocks need to be logically connected for the sentence to make sense. Likewise, it does not make sense to write the following sentence:

Emphasis on WHY

Ex.: ***Because he likes the view****, Léandre will buy a penthouse in New York City through a real estate agent.*

WHY **WHO** **WHAT**

WHERE **HOW**

Your Sentence

The above sentence does not make sense either the WHY is disconnected from the HOW. It is the same sentence as above, but the order of information was reversed. Now, let's assume that the HOW and the WHY are indeed connected. We can still run into another problem in constructing a sentence. That problem is **style**.

Emphasis on WHY

Ex.: ***Because he is lazy****, Léandre will buy a penthouse in New York City through a real estate agent.*

WHY **WHO** **WHAT**

WHERE **HOW**

Your Sentence

The sentence above works well because after the WHY is emphasized comes the WHO and the WHAT and then comes the HOW. But things can go wrong fast if we don't pay careful attention to our information blocks.

Emphasis on WHY

Ex.: ***Because he is lazy****, through a real estate agent, Léandre will buy a penthouse in New York City.*

WHY **HOW** **WHO**

WHAT **WHERE**

Your Sentence

The above sentence <u>doesn't</u> sound right because we've put too many information blocks before the WHO and the WHAT.

Avoid stuffing your sentence with information blocks before your WHO and the WHAT. Your readers need to know the WHO and the WHAT rapidly or else they will get confused.

Emphasis on WHO and WHAT

Ex.: ***Léandre will buy a penthouse*** *in New York City through a real estate agent because he is lazy.*

WHO **WHAT** **WHERE**

HOW **WHY**

The sentence above works well because the HOW and the WHY logically follow one another after the WHO and the WHAT. As you develop your writing skills, it will become easier for you to know where exactly to place each information block. The best way you can improve rapidly is by reading texts thinking about information blocks. Read for information blocks and ask yourself why they are ordered the way they are.

There is one information block we haven't yet addressed, and that information block is TO WHOM. You'll remember from Lesson 2 that a sentence must have someone doing something. This is to say, a sentence must have a *character* and an *action.* Most of the time, the action is made of **two** word roles: a **verb** and a **direct object**. But in some cases, someone receives the action, which means the action is made by the **subject** for the **indirect object**, the receiver of the action.

Ex.: Léandre will give a penthouse ***to his girlfriend.***

WHO **WHAT** **TO WHOM**

In the sentence above, Léandre makes the action of giving a New York City penthouse to his girlfriend. As other information blocks, TO WHOM can be moved around in the sentence.

Your Sentence

Ex.: Léandre will give ***his girlfriend*** *a penthouse.*

WHO	TO WHOM	WHAT

The above sentence means the exact same thing as the other one, but it is stylistically different because of the order.

Your Sentence

____

____

Now that you understand the different information blocks, their word roles, and their parts of speech, you need to understand the other layers of a sentence. The other components of the sentences are **phrases** and **clauses**, and they are critical in understanding sentence structure.

Lesson 4

Not All Information Blocks Are Created Equal

***In a way, clauses are small sentences because they have a WHO and a WHAT. But there are two types of clauses:* dependent *and* independent.**

The variables in your dream aren't equally significant.

Think about what you need to achieve your dream. There are different pieces of information necessary to its realization. There are different variables at play, too. Some variables must be dependent, and some must be independent.

What this means is that for some things to happen, some other things need to happen first. For example, if you dream of owning a house, you need to have access to capital. Without capital, you cannot own a house. In this case, owning a house is dependent on your ability to access capital.

The same is true in writing. The different pieces of information are **phrases** and the variables are **clauses**. The different pieces of information give us context inside the variables.

In this lesson, you will

- Learn about **phrases** and how they convey information
- Learn about **clauses** and how to connect ideas together

Phrases Convey Information

Phrases are groups of words that function together as a part of speech would. Phrases take their name from the part of speech they are based on. (Note that determiners alone are not a phrase because they qualify nouns.)

Phrase Type	Definitions	Examples
Noun phrase	Group of words which function together as a **noun**.	"the penthouse," "the beautiful penthouse," or "the extremely beautiful penthouse."
Verbal phrase	Group of words which function together as a **verb**.	"is searching," "can go," "could have done," "must see," etc.
Adjective phrase	Group of words which function together as an **adjective**.	"overly enthusiastic," "very small," "who seems upset," etc.
Adverbial phrase	Group of words which function together as an **adverb**.	"right here," "right here by the garage," etc.
Prepositional phrase	Group of words which function together as a **preposition**	"with the black hat," "on the table," "by my car," "toward my place," etc.
Conjunctional phrase	Group of words which function together as a **conjunction**.	"as soon as," "as quickly as," "neither you nor I," etc.

Clauses Show Relationships Between Simple Ideas

One of the most important information blocks in a sentence are clauses. In a way, clauses are small sentences because they have a subject and a verb (a WHO and a WHAT.) But there are two types of clauses: **dependent** and **independent.** Although independent clauses can be sentences, dependent clauses cannot because the rely on the independent clause to make sense.

Independent Clause —— *Dependent Clause* ————

Ex.: Léandre has a mortgage because he bought a penthouse.

In other words, clauses are simple ideas, made of multiple phrases, that provide more than one piece of information (WHO, WHAT, WHERE, WHOSE, WHEN, HOW, and WHY).

Independent clauses	Part of a sentence that <u>can</u> stand on its own.	"Léandre bought a penthouse."
Dependent clauses	Part of a sentence that <u>cannot</u> stand on its own.	"Because Léandre bought a penthouse."
Defining relative clauses	Part of a sentence that adds <u>necessary</u> information.	"The real estate agent **who helped Léandre** did a good job."
Non-Defining relative clauses	Part of a sentence that adds <u>unnecessary</u> information	"The real estate agent, **who took care of everything**, made a lot of money."

As you can see from the examples above, only a **dependent clause** can stand on its own as a sentence. That's because a dependent clause requires a **conjunction**, and conjunctions introduce a condition before the action. Although a dependent clause does have a subject and a verb (a WHO and a WHAT), it cannot happen on its own, which makes it dependent on the independent clause.

In the next lesson, we will focus more specifically on what goes inside clauses. To do so, we will be looking at phrases and word roles.

Part II

Clauses

Lesson 5

Clauses Make or Break Sentences

Without an independent clause, you do not have a sentence.

Your dream must have an independent variable.

In the last lesson, we talked about independent and dependent clauses. Think about it this way: If your dream only had one dependent variable, it would never work, correct? Remember, "because he bought a penthouse" doesn't work if Léandre doesn't "have a mortgage". Buying a penthouse leads to the mortgage, meaning it is it the condition for the mortgage.

But if your dream only had one dependent variable, it would not work. It would simply serve something greater, and it would not be great itself. For example, making money is a dependent variable because has no significance alone. The things money can buy give money its significance.

If your dream is only to make money (**dependent variable**) and you don't plan to spend it (**independent variable**), you don't have a dream. The same goes for writing: Without an independent clause, you do not have a sentence.

In this lesson, you will

- Learn what makes a clause **dependent** or **independent**
- See some examples of how **clauses** make or break sentences

Dependent clauses make the information they contain (WHO and WHAT) dependent on what comes next through a conjunction. In other words, they delay the *real* action in the sentence. Here is a short list of conjunctions that make clauses dependent:

After	Once
Although	Now that
As	Since
As long as	Though
Because	Unless
Before	Until
Even if	When
If	While

I cannot overemphasize this: It is as important to have at least one independent clause in a sentence as it is important to have someone doing something. Without an independent clause, your readers won't understand what you are trying to communicate to them.

Read the following sentences:

After Léandre bought a penthouse.

Unless Léandre bought a penthouse.

Although Léandre bought a penthouse.

Since Léandre bought a penthouse.

These sentences have a WHO and WHAT, but they do not make sense because they imply that something should come after. That's because they only contain a dependent clause each. In contrast, read the following sentences:

After Léandre bought a penthouse, a real estate market crash occurred in the city.

Since Léandre bought a penthouse, the coffee shops in the neighborhood have seen an increase in sales.

Although Léandre bought a penthouse, the real estate prices in the city did not increase.

Unless Léandre bought a penthouse, the city would not be as exciting.

These sentences actually make sense because they have both a dependent and an independent clause. The dependent clause shows the condition for the independent clause to happen. **What truly matters is the independent clause.**

If we remove its dependent clause, a sentence might lose some of its meaning, but it would still make sense and be grammatically correct. But if we remove its independent clause, a sentence makes no sense and is grammatically incorrect. In the sentences above, the dependent clause is about Léandre and the independent clause about something else that happens.

Now that you know the two different types of clauses available and their effect, you need to understand the components that make up these clauses. To do so, we need to dig deeper into the word roles, which give meaning to clauses. What you are about to learn in the next lesson applies both to dependent and independent clauses.

Lesson 6

Clauses Are Made of Subjects and Objects

No dream is great if it doesn't involve other people. If you have a big dream, you need to involve other people in it.

Most often, your dream doesn't involve just you, the subject, but also others, the objects.

No dream is great if it doesn't involve other people. If you have a big dream, you need to involve other people in it. Every step of the way, you need to interact with other people. The same is true in writing sentences: clauses include you, the **subject** (the WHO) and other people, the **objects** (part of the WHAT).

What you are learning in this lesson applies to both dependent and independent clauses. It's time to see the basics in action! (If you feel confused by any grammatical term or abbreviation, visit the glossary at the end of this book.)

In this lesson, you will

- Explore clauses with no **direct object**
- Explore clauses with a **direct object**
- **Passive voice** in a clause
- **Possessives** in a clause

Clauses Without a Direct Object

Some sentences don't involve anyone else other than the **subject**. That's because they use an **intransitive verb**. Intransitive verbs make sense on their own; they do not need a **direct object**. These sentences are like dreams achieved alone. Although correct, they are not the majority of sentences.

Below, you can see the breakdown of a clause without a **direct object**. On the left-side column, you can see the different levels of the sentence: 1) the question words (QW); 2) the clauses (CL); 3) the phrases (PH); 4) the word roles (WR); and 5) and the parts of speech (POS). Sentences can be analyzed in all these different ways.

1.	*WHO*	*WHAT*
2.	*Independent clause*	
3.		*Verb phrase*
	Léandre	**arrived**.
4.	*Subject*	*Verb*
5.	*Noun*	*Instransitive Verb*

Your Sentence

____

____

Clause with a Direct Object

Most sentences involve a direct object, which is either a person or a physical object. Sentences need a direct object when they have a *transitive* verb. You know that a verb is intransitive because, by itself, it leaves you wondering, "what?" When a sentence uses a transitive verb, the WHAT of a sentence is made of both a **verb** and a **direct object**. These sentences are like dreams that involve other people or things.

1.	*WHO* ——	*WHAT* ————————		
2.	*Independent clause* ————————			
3.		*Verb Phrase*	*Noun phrase* ———	
	Léandre	**bought**	**the**	**penthouse**.
4.	*Subject*	*Verb*	*direct object*	
5.	*Noun*	*Verb*	*Def. Art*	*Noun*

Your Sentence

Clauses With Passive Voice

More often than not, your subject should come first in your clause. Why? Because the subject is the most important thing. It's the character, and people read about characters.

But sometimes, we need to place the direct object first because it's actually more important than the subject. We call this "passive voice," and it should only be used for the following reason:

- We need to exceptionally emphasize the direct object of the sentence
- We need to hide the subject to create an effect
- We are trying to minimize blame on the subject

(Direct Object) (Verb) (Subject)

Ex.: The penthouse was bought by Léandre.

WHAT	WHO

1. *WHAT* —— *WHO* ——
2. *Independent clause* ——
3. *Noun phrase* — *Verb phrase*

The penthouse was bought by Léandre.

4. *Direct Object* *Verb*—— *Subject*
5. *Def. Art* *Noun* *Verb* —— *Prep.* *Noun*

When you use the passive voice, you place the emphasis on the object rather than the subject. Moreover, your verb requires a minimum of two words. It makes your writing heavier and more complicated, but it is sometimes fair to use it. Many people overuse the passive voice, and it hinders their writing. Use the passive voice deliberately to fulfill a purpose.

Your Sentence

Clauses With an Indirect Object

Sometimes, the subjects of a sentence don't take an action for themselves but for someone else. This "someone else" is the indirect object, and it receives the action made by the subject. The **direct object** is the recipient of the **verb** in the sentence, while the **indirect object** is the recipient of the **direct object**.

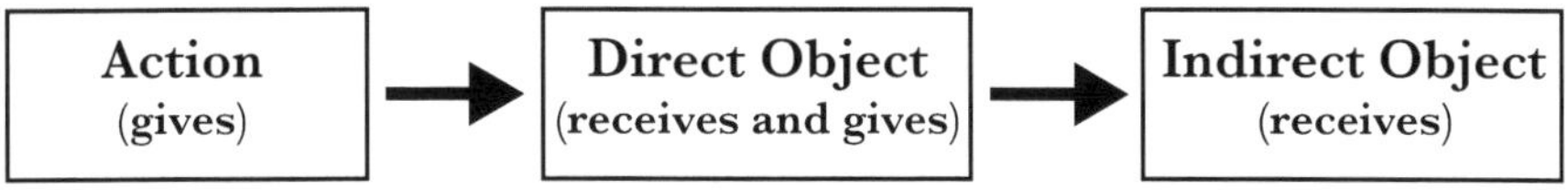

Sentences are chains of giving and receiving. Think about it this way: the **verb** (performed by the subject) gives to the **direct object**, and the **direct object** gives to the **indirect object.**

1. *WHO* *WHAT* *TO WHOM*— *WHAT*——

2. *Independent clause* ——————————

3. *Verb Ph.* *Noun phrase* *Noun phrase* —

Léandre bought his girlfriend the penthouse.

4. *Subject* *Verb* *Indirect Obj.* *Direct Object*

5. *Noun* *Verb* *Pr. Noun* *Def. Art.* *Noun*

Your Sentence

___

___

Clauses with Possessives

The nouns in a sentence have relationships with one another, and sometimes a noun belongs to another. It's important to clearly show these relationships of belonging for sentences to be clear.

The possessive form is used to indicate that something belongs to someone. When using the possessive form, we use two nouns. However, they become part of the same noun phrase and the same word role. We commonly form the possessive with an apostrophe (') and a -s.

1.	*WHO*		*WHAT*	
2.	*Independent clause*			
3.	*Noun phrase*		*Verb ph.*	*Noun phrase*
	Léandre's	**girlfriend**	**bought**	**the penthouse**.
4.	*Subject*		*Verb*	*Direct Object*
5.	*Noun*	*Noun*	*Verb*	*Def. Art Noun*

Your Sentence

____

____

Now that you've explored clauses without a direct object, with a direct object, with the passive voice, and with possessives, you are ready to explore clauses with different phrases.

Lesson 7

Noun, Verb, and Adjective Phrases Fill Clauses with Characters and Actions

Sometimes, our characters and actions are more complicated than parts of speech; they are phrases, which means they are group of words playing the role of the characters and actions.

The characters and actions of your dream are often more complicated than they appear.

In previous lessons, we've talked about nouns and verbs. Remember, these are the characters (WHO) and actions (WHAT) in our sentences. But **nouns** and **verbs** are simple characters and actions; they are parts of speech. Sometimes, our characters and actions are more complicated than parts of speech; they are phrases, which means they are groups of words playing the roles of the characters and actions.

In this lesson, you will

- Learn how to use noun phrases in a clause
- Learn how to use verb phrases in a clause
- Learn how to use adjective phrases in a clause

Noun Phrases in a Clause

A noun phrase is a group of words that acts as a noun. Sentences almost always contain a **noun phrase** because nouns require articles much of the time (e.g., "a" and "the"). If the subject is a proper noun (e.g., Léandre) or a common noun in the plural form (e.g., cats), then no article is necessary. Most of the time, a noun will require the article "a" or "the," which turns the noun into a noun phrase.

A noun phrase allows you to add details to a noun. For example, you can add an adjective, which *qualifies* the noun. If you add an adjective, you are adding another part of speech and therefore adding to the **noun phrase.**

1. Independent clause ————————————

2. Noun Phrase ———— *Verb phrase* *Noun phrase* ————

The young Canadian bought a penthouse.

3. Subject ———— *Verb* *Direct Object* ————

4. Def. Art. *Adj* *Noun* *Verb* *Ind. Art* *Noun*

Your Sentence

____

____

Adjectives can qualify not only subjects but also direct objects and indirect objects.

1. Independent clause ————————————

2. Noun Phrase ———— *Verb ph.* *Noun phrase* ————

The young Canadian bought a beautiful penthouse.

3. Subject ———— *Verb* *Direct Object* ————

4. Def. Art. Adj *Noun* *Verb* *Ind. Art* *Adj.* *Noun*

Your Sentence

____

____

1. *Independent clause* ——————————————

2. *Noun Phrase* ———— *Verb p.* *Noun phrase* ——— *Noun phrase* —

The young Canadian bought his beautiful girlfriend a penthouse.

3. *Subject* ———— *Verb* *Indirect Object* ——— *Direct Object*

4. *D.A. Adj.* *Noun* *Verb* *Pr.* *Adj.* *Noun* *I.A.* *Noun*

Your Sentence

____

____

If you list multiple adjectives in a noun phrase, they must be in the following order:

- Quantity or number
- Quality or opinion
- Size
- Age
- Shape
- Color
- Proper adjective (often nationality, other place of origin, or material)
- Purpose or qualifier

*Ex.: A **friendly 35-year-old Canadian** man bought the penthouse.*

Your Sentence

____

____

(Note that "35-year-old" is a compound adjective, which is why we use hyphens. More on hyphens in the punctuation section.)

If you want to add even more detail to the noun, you can add an adverb to the adjective. Although adverbs normally qualify verbs, they also modify adjectives to add more details.

Ex.: ***The extremely young Canadian*** *bought a penthouse.*

Your Sentence

Verb Phrases in a Clause

A verb phrase is a group of words that acts as a verb. Just like characters (WHO), actions (WHAT) can be more than one part of speech. To describe an action, we sometimes use multiple verbs, which creates a verb phrase.

Ex.: Léandre ***is buying*** *the penthouse.*

Ex.: Léandre ***might buy*** *the penthouse.*

Your Sentence

The different verbs used in the sentences above show nuances in the action. In the first one, "is buying" shows that the action is currently ongoing. In the second one, "might buy" shows that the character is not sure of completing the action.

Adjective Phrases in a Clause

If you add adjectives to a noun, you create a noun phrase. But if you stack adjectives on top of one another, you create adjective phrases.

*Ex.: **Ready and eager**, Léandre bought the beautiful penthouse.*

Your Sentence

____

____

*Ex.: Léandre is **ready and eager** to buy the beautiful penthouse.*

Your Sentence

____

____

Now that you've learned how to use noun, verb, and adjective phrase, you're ready to learn about how to use adverbs and adverbial phrases.

Lesson 8

Adverbs and Adverbial Phrases Change the Clause's Action

When we modify verbs, we modify the meaning of a sentence because the action takes place in a different context

The actions of your dream depend on the context in which they are located.

If we added, removed, or changed pieces of information in your dream, it wouldn't be the same, would it? For example, if you did an action in a different place, at a different time, or for a different reason, the dream would be different. The same is true of writing: If you add, remove, or change components to your sentence, its meaning changes. However, some components, such as adverbs and adverbial phrases, are subtle in how they change a sentence's meaning.

In this lesson, you will

- Explore how **adverbs** and **adverbial phrases** change a clause's action
- See examples of how we use **adverbs** and **adverbial phrases** in different locations within a sentence

In the same way adjectives modify nouns, **adverbs** modify verbs—as well as adjectives or other adverbs. When we modify verbs, we modify the meaning of a sentence because the action takes place in a different context.

Unlike with adjectives, the position of an **adverb** may vary from one sentence to another. Sometimes it's placed before the verb while other times it's placed after. It depends on what it is we are trying to say.

Ex.: Léandre ***confidently*** *buys a penthouse in New York City.*

Your Sentence

____

____

Ex.: Léandre sits ***comfortably*** *on the couche in his new penthouse.*

Your Sentence

____

____

Adverbs come in different shapes and forms. There are five different types of **adverbs**, all of which serve to express the answers to different sentence questions: the WHEN, WHERE, WHY, HOW, and HOW OFTEN.

As you'll see, an **adverbial phrase** uses several words to modify a verb, an adjective or an adverb—rather than with just one, like with **adverbs** do. These parts of the sentence are moveable across a sentence depending on the emphasis we wish to give them. Their position, in effect, changes the meaning of the sentence.

Note that adverbial phrases can appear in different formats, such as prepositional phrases, infinitive phrases, etc. As we go through adverbs and adverbial phrases, we will start looking at different versions of the same sentence to highlight the different meanings possible.

Remember that information is always given in order of relevance: what comes first is the most important and what comes last is the least important.

Adverbs of time

Adverbs of time are **words** that help express the WHEN.

Placed at the Beginning

*Ex.: **Yesterday**, Léandre bought a penthouse.*

By placing the adverb of time at the beginning, you are putting emphasis on the WHEN.

Your Sentence

Placed at the End

*Ex.: Léandre bought a penthouse **yesterday**.*

By placing the adverb of time at the end, you are putting emphasis on the WHO and the WHAT.

Your Sentence

Adverbial phrases of time

Adverbial phrases of time are **phrases** that help express the WHEN.

Placed at the Beginning

*Ex.: **Last year**, Léandre bought a penthouse.*

By placing the adverbial phrase of time at the beginning, you are putting emphasis on the WHEN.

Your Sentence

Placed at the End

*Ex.: Léandre bought a penthouse **last year**.*

By placing the adverbial phrase of time at the end, you are putting emphasis on the WHO and the WHAT.

Your Sentence

Adverbs of place

Adverbs of place are **words** that help express the WHERE.

Placed at the Beginning

*Ex.: **Here**, Léandre bought a penthouse.*

By placing the **adverb of place** at the beginning, you are putting emphasis on the WHERE.

Your Sentence

Placed at the End

Ex.: Léandre bought a penthouse ***here****.*

By placing the **adverb of place** at the end, you are putting emphasis on the WHO and the WHAT.

Your Sentence

Adverbial phrases of place

Adverbial phrases of place are **phrases** that help express the WHERE.

Placed at the Beginning

Ex.: ***In New York City,*** *Léandre bought a penthouse.*

By placing the **adverbial phrase of place** at the beginning, you are putting emphasis on the WHERE.

Your Sentence

Placed at the End

Ex.: Léandre bought a penthouse ***in New York City****.*

By placing the **adverbial phrase of place** at the end, you are putting emphasis on the WHO and the WHAT.

Your Sentence

Adverbs of frequency

Adverbs of frequency are **words** that help express the HOW OFTEN.

Placed at the Beginning

Ex.: ***Sometimes**, Léandre buys houses.*

By placing the **adverb of frequency** at the beginning, you are putting emphasis on the HOW OFTEN.

Your Sentence

Placed in the Middle

*Ex.: Léandre **sometimes** buys houses.*

By placing the **adverb of frequency** in the middle, you are putting emphasis on the WHO.

Your Sentence

Placed at the End

Ex.: ***Léandre** buys houses sometimes.*

By placing the **adverb of frequency** at the end, you are putting emphasis on the WHO and WHAT.

Your Sentence

Adverbial phrases of frequency

Adverbial phrases of frequency are **phrases** that help express the HOW OFTEN.

Placed at the Beginning

*Ex.: **Every year**, Léandre buys a house.*

By placing the **adverbial phrase of frequency** at the beginning, you are putting emphasis on the HOW OFTEN.

Your Sentence

Placed in the End

*Ex.: Léandre buys a house **every year**.*

By placing the **adverbial phrase of frequency** at the end, you are putting emphasis on the WHO and WHAT.

Your Sentence

Adverbs of manner

Adverbs of manner are **words** that help express the HOW.

Placed at the Beginning

*Ex.: **Eagerly**, Léandre bought a house.*

By placing the **adverb of manner** at the beginning, you are putting emphasis on the HOW.

Your Sentence

____

____

Placed in the End

*Ex.: Léandre bought a house **eagerly**.*

By placing the **adverb of manner** at the end, you are putting emphasis on the WHO and WHAT.

Your Sentence

____

____

Adverbial phrases of manner

Adverbial phrases of manner are **phrases** that help express the HOW.

Placed at the Beginning

*Ex.: **Without hesitation**, Léandre bought a house.*

By placing the **adverb of manner** at the beginning, you are putting emphasis on the HOW.

Your Sentence

____

____

Placed in the Middle

*Ex.: Léandre, **without hesitation**, bought a house in New York City.*

By placing the **adverb of manner** in the middle, you are putting emphasis on the WHO.

Your Sentence

____

____

Placed at the End

*Ex.: Léandre bought a house **without hesitation**.*

By placing the **adverb of manner** at the end, you are putting emphasis on the WHO and WHAT.

Your Sentence

____

____

Adverbs of degree

Adverbs of degree are **words** that help express the HOW.

Placed Before the Verb

*Ex.: Léandre **almost** bought two houses.*

By placing the **adverb of manner** before the verb, you are making it modify the action.

Your Sentence

____

____

Placed Before the Direct Object

*Ex.: Léandre bought **almost** two houses.*

By placing the **adverb of degree** before the direct object, you are making it modify the direct object.

Your Sentence

____

____

Adverb of reason

Adverbs of reason are **words** that help express the WHY.

Placed at the Beginning

*Ex.: **Therefore**, Léandre almost bought two houses.*

By placing the **adverb of reason** at the beginning, you are putting the emphasis on the WHY.

Your Sentence

____

____

Placed in the Middle

*Ex.: Léandre, **therefore**, almost bought two houses.*

By placing the **adverb of reason** in the middle, you are putting the emphasis on the WHO.

Your Sentence

____

____

Adverbial phrases of reason

Adverbial phrases of reason are **phrases** that help express the WHY.

Placed at the Beginning

Ex.: ***As a result**, Léandre almost bought two houses.*

By placing the **adverbial phrase of reason** at the beginning, you are putting the emphasis on the WHY.

Your Sentence

____

____

Placed in the Middle

Ex.: Léandre, ***as a result**, almost bought two houses.*

By placing the **adverbial phrase of reason** in the middle, you are putting the emphasis on the WHO.

Your Sentence

____

____

Placed at the End

Ex.: Léandre almost bought two houses ***as a result**.*

By placing the **adverbial phrase of reason** at the end, you are putting the emphasis on the WHO and WHAT.

Your Sentence

____

____

Now that you understand how to use **adverbs** and **adverbial phrases** in clauses, you are ready to dig deeper and start understanding **phrases** in a different way.

Lesson 9

Prepositional, Infinitive, Absolute, and Appositive Phrases in a Clause

Noun phrases play the role of a noun and adverbial phrases play the role of an adverb. What we didn't talk about, however, is that other phrases can play these roles through other means.

In the last lessons, we've focused on phrases that play the role they are named after. For example, noun phrases play the role of a noun and adverbial phrases play the role of an adverb. What we didn't talk about, however, is that other phrases can play these roles through other means.

In the next few lessons, we will look at phrases in another way. We will look not at the phrases that play the role they are named after, but rather the phrases named after the part of speech they use. We will look at prepositional, infinitive, participial, absolute, and gerund phrases. These phrases can play roles their names do not indicate.

In this lesson, you will

- Learn how to use prepositional phrases in a clause both as a noun and as an adjective
- Explore conjunctional phrases in a clause
- Explore participial, absolute, and appositive phrases in a clause
- Learn about using different verb tenses in a clause

Prepositional Phrases in a Clause

Prepositions show relationships between words and give pieces of information such as time and place. Prepositional phrases, as their name indicates, use prepositions to convey meaning. They can play the role of a **noun**, **adjective**, or **adverb**. Here are some common prepositions:

According to the judge	**Like** a child
Across different countries	**Near** the ocean
After many arrests	**Off** the grid
Against the world	**On** the table
Amid the chaos	**Through** the window
Around the city	**Throughout** the thick forest
Before we proceeded to the arrest	**To** the beach
Between a rock and a hard place	**Under** the radar

Prepositional Phrase as a Noun

When acting as a noun, the prepositional phrase acts as a noun and is followed by a **linking verb** (is).

*Ex.: **In a penthouse** is where Léandre wants to be.*

Your Sentence

____

____

Prepositional Phrase as an Adjective

When acting as an adjective, the prepositional phrase can modify either the **subject** or the **direct object**, or the **indirect object.**

Modifying the Subject

Ex.: The penthouse ***on the corner of 7th Ave. and W. 37th St.*** *is the property Léandre wants to buy.*

In this sentence, the penthouse is the subject, not the direct object, and the prepositional phrase acts as an adjective that modifies it and expresses the WHERE.

Your Sentence

____

____

Modifying the Direct Object

Ex.: The 7th Ave. penthouse is a property **under the radar**.

In this sentence, the prepositional phrase acts as an adjective that modifies the direct object (a property) and expresses the WHAT.

Your Sentence

____

____

Conjunctional Phrases in a Clause

Conjunctions link words, phrases, and clauses together. Conjunctional phrases, as their name indicates, use conjunctions to convey meaning. There are different types of conjunctions.

In this section, we will only cover one type of conjunctional phrases, those using <u>correlative conjunctions</u>. We won't cover the other types of conjunctions yet as other types of conjunctions lead us to dependent clauses, which we will cover in the lesson on complex sentences.

Here are a few examples of <u>correlative conjunctions</u>, which work together in a team to establish the relationship between a pair of words:

Both/and	Neither/nor
Whether/or	Not/but
Either/or	Not only/but also

Ex.: ***Both*** *Léandre* ***and*** *his girlfriend want to buy the 7th Ave. penthouse.*

Your Sentence

___

___

Ex.: Léandre does not care ***whether*** *the penthouse is overpriced* ***or*** *not.*

Your Sentence

___

___

Ex.: Léandre wants ***either*** *the 7th Ave. penthouse* ***or*** *the 5th Ave. penthouse.*

Your Sentence

___

___

Ex.: ***Neither*** *Léandre* ***nor*** *his girlfriend wants to lose this opportunity.*

Your Sentence

___

___

Ex.: Léandre wants ***not*** *any penthouse* ***but*** *this penthouse.*

Your Sentence

___

___

Infinitive Phrases in a Clause

Infinitive phrases use an infinitive verb (e.g., to be) to play their role, namely, that of a **noun** (WHO, WHAT), an **adjective** (WHAT), or an **adverb** (HOW, HOW OFTEN).

As a noun

In the following sentences, the infinitive phrases become part of the noun phrases since it plays the role of a noun. However, the information it gives depends on whether it is the subject or the direct object.

As the Subject (WHO)

*Ex.: **To buy the penthouse** is Léandre's goal.*

Your Sentence

____

____

As the Direct Object (WHAT)

*Ex.: Léandre's goal is **to buy the penthouse**.*

Your Sentence

____

____

As an Adjective

*Ex.: The best penthouse **to view Manhattan's skyline** is the one on 7th Ave.*

Your Sentence

____

____

As an Adverb

*Ex.: Léandre charmed the real estate agent **to get the penthouse.***

Your Sentence

____

____

Gerund Phrases in a Simple Sentence

Gerund sentences are phrases using gerund verbs, namely, verbs ending with "-ing".

Placed at the Beginning

Ex.: ***Charming the real estate agent**, Léandre got a deal.*

Your Sentence

____

____

Placed in the Middle

Ex.: Léandre, ***charming the real estate agent**, got a deal.*

Your Sentence

____

____

Placed at the End

Ex.: Léandre got a deal ***charming the real estate agent**.*

Your Sentence

____

____

Participial Phrases in a Clause

Participial phrases are phrases that use **past participles**, namely, verbs that finish either by "–d," "-ed," "-n," "-en," or "–t," or the present participle, namely, verbs that finish by "-ing." The participial phrase always acts as an adjective.

Placed at the Beginning

Ex.: ***Charmed by Léandre**, the real estate agent accepted the deal.*

Your Sentence

____

____

Placed at the End

Ex.: The real estate agent accepted the deal ***taken aback***

Your Sentence

____

____

Placed in the Middle

Ex.: The real estate agent, ***forgetting how to negotiate****, accepted the deal.*

Your Sentence

____

____

Absolute Phrases in a Simple Sentence

Unlike other phrases, which generally modify a specific part of the sentence, **absolute phrases** modify the whole sentence—thus they are non-essential to the sentence.

Placed at the Beginning

Ex.: ***His deal closed****, Léandre went to get a drink.*

Your Sentence

____

____

Placed at the End

Ex.: Léandre went to get a drink, ***his excitement being higher than ever****.*

Your Sentence

____

____

Appositive Phrases in a Clause

Appositive phrases are nouns or noun phrases, set off by commas, that rename the noun or the pronoun it precedes.

Placed in the Beginning

Ex.: ***The writing coach****, Léandre Larouche, bought the penthouse.*

Your Sentence

____

____

Placed in the Middle

Ex.: Léandre Larouche, ***the writing coach****, bought the penthouse.*

Your Sentence

____

____

Placed at the End

Ex.: The penthouse bought by Léandre Larouche, ***the writing coach****.*

Your Sentence

____

____

Using different verb tenses in a clause

So far, we've used the past tense for this sentence for convenience. Changing the verb tense does not alter the general word order in a clause. However, certain verb tenses may require you to add an indicator of time or information to create a meaningful sentence.

Here are the main verb tenses in the English language:

- **Present Simple**: I do

The present tense indicates that something is the case right now. However, it does not always mean it is happening right now. When we use the present tense, we sometimes have to clarify when the action happens as in the sentence below.

Ex.: Léandre ***buys*** *a penthouse today.*

Your Sentence

- **Present Continuous**: I am doing

The present continuous indicates that something is occurring right now.

Ex.: Léandre ***is buying*** *a penthouse right now.*

Your Sentence

- **Present Perfect**: I have done

The present perfect indicates that something was done at an uncertain point in time in the past.

Ex.: Léandre ***has bought*** *a penthouse.*

Your Sentence

- **Present Perfect Continuous**: I have been doing

The present perfect continuous means that something has started in the past and is still currently ongoing.

Ex.: Léandre ***has been buying*** *penthouses this year.*

Your Sentence

- **Past Simple:** I did

The past simple indicates that something happened at a specific time in the past. Often, it requires a time marker (e.g., yesterday).

Ex.: Léandre ***bought*** *a penthouse last night.*

Your Sentence

- **Past Continuous**: I was doing

The past continuous indicates something was currently ongoing at a specified moment in time. Often, it requires a time marker (e.g., yesterday).

Ex.: Léandre ***was buying*** *a penthouse last night.*

Your Sentence

- **Past Perfect**: I had done

The past perfect indicates that something occurred before another something else which is to follow in the sentence.

Ex.: Léandre ***had bought*** *a penthouse when the real estate market crash happened.*

Your Sentence

- **Past Perfect Continuous**: I had been doing

The past perfect continuous indicates that something had been ongoing before something (which follows in the sentence) occurred.

Ex.: Léandre ***had been buying*** *penthouses when the real estate market crash happened.*

Your Sentence

- **Future Simple**: I will do

  The future simple indicates that something will occur in the future.

*Ex.: Léandre **will buy** a penthouse tomorrow.*

Your Sentence

___

___

- **Future Perfect:** I will have done

  The future perfect indicates that at a certain point, something will already have occurred.

*Ex.: Léandre **will have bought** a penthouse by the time you get home.*

Your Sentence

___

___

- **Future Perfect Continuous**: I will have been doing

  The future perfect continuous indicates that after a certain point (which is to be indicated in the sentence) something else will already be ongoing.

*Ex.: Léandre **will have been buying** penthouses for ten years when he turns forty.*

Your Sentence

___

___

Now that you've learned what goes inside clauses, you need to learn which types of clauses to use and when to use them based on the type of sentence you are writing. To this end, we turn to sentence structure in the next section.

Part III

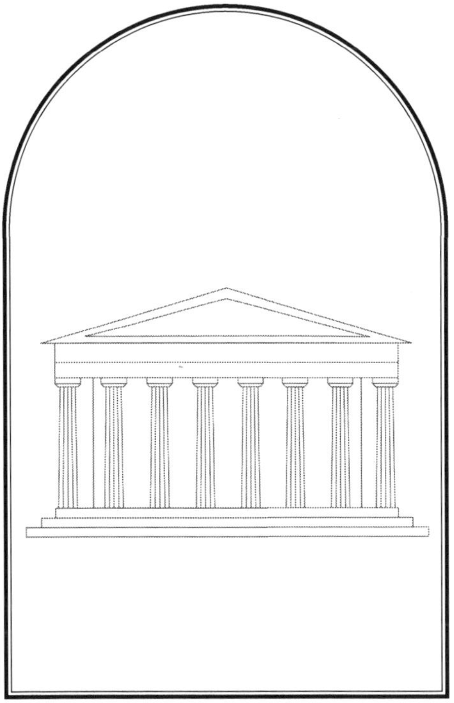

Sentence Structure

Lesson 10

A Simple Sentence Has One Independent Clause

A* simple sentence *is made of an independent clause only, and the independent clause (*Subject + Verb + Object*) is the basic requirement for any grammatical sentence.

A simple dream has only one independent variable.

If you can achieve your dream without any external condition, it's a simple dream. There's nothing wrong with that, but it's a simple dream. It is what it is, and it's straightforward. You can't miss it or confuse it with something it's not. The same thing is true of sentences: The most simple and commonest type of sentence is the simple sentence.

In this lesson, you will

- Learn what a **simple sentence** is
- Learn what a **sentence fragment** is

A **simple sentence** is made of an independent clause only, and the independent clause (**Subject** + **Verb** + **Object**) is the basic requirement for any grammatical sentence. Remember that without the subject or the verb, you don't have a complete sentence; you have a **fragment**. Fragments are ungrammatical most of the time. As we will see later, there are only few occasions where fragments are acceptable.

Simple Sentence

Ex.: Léandre bought the penthouse.

Your Sentence

____

____

Sentence Fragments

Ex.: Léandre bought.

Ex.: The penthouse.

Now that you know what simple sentences and sentence fragments are, you are ready to learn about the complex sentence!

Lesson 11

A Complex Sentence Has One Independent Clause and One Dependent Clause

A complex sentence is made of both an independent clause and at least one dependent clause. Complex sentences take different names depending on which clause comes first.

A complex dream has not only an independent variable, but also a dependent variable.

The more dependent variables your dream has, the more complex it is. Why? Because it requires more steps before your dream comes true. The same is true of writing: Dependent clauses are steps we must take before getting to the independent clause.

In this lesson, you will

- Learn what a **complex sentence** is
- Learn the two different types of complex sentences (**loose** and **periodic**) and how to use them

A complex sentence is made of both an **independent clause** and at least one **dependent clause.** They have one or many clauses that can't stand on their own (dependent) and one that can stand on its own (independent). Be careful to use dependent clauses in moderation as they make your writing more complex, which means more difficult to read.

Ex.: After Léandre bought a penthouse, a real estate market crash occurred in the city.

Dependent clause:

After Léandre bought a penthouse,

Independent clause:

a real estate market crash occurred in the city.

Complex sentences take different names depending on which clause comes first. If the independent clause comes first, we are dealing with a **loose sentence**. If the independent clause comes last, we are dealing with a **periodic sentence**. Good writing relies primarily on periodic sentences. You should have about 1 loose sentence for every 5 periodic sentences.

Periodic Sentences

A periodic sentence is a complex sentence in which the **independent clause** (main point) comes **last**. It is a strong sentence and good writing primarily relies on periodic sentences when using complex sentences.

Ex.: ***After Léandre bought a penthouse****, a real estate market crash occurred in the city.*

Dependent clause:

After Léandre bought a penthouse,

Independent clause:

a real estate market crash occurred in the city.

Your Sentence

____

____

Loose Sentences

A loose sentence is a complex sentence in which the **independent clause** (main point) comes **first**. It is not a strong sentence, and it can weaken your writing if overused. However, it is welcome and necessary to vary your writing.

Ex.: A real estate market crash occurred ***after Léandre bought a penthouse****.*

Dependent clause:

A real estate market crash occurred

Independent clause:

after Léandre bought a penthouse.

Your Sentence

____

____

This is worth restating: Good writing relies primarily on periodic sentences. You should have about 1 loose sentence for every 5 periodic sentences.

Multiple Dependent Clauses in a Complex Sentence

You can have more than one dependent clause in a complex sentence. However, remember that the more dependent clauses you have, the more complex your sentence becomes.

Ex.: ***After Léandre bought a penthouse****, but before the economy crashed, a real estate market crash occurred in the city.*

Dependent clause:

After Léandre bought a penthouse

Dependent clause:

but before the economy crashed,

Independent clause:

a real estate market crash occurred in the city.

Your Sentence

Ex.: A real estate market crash occurred in the city after Léandre bought a penthouse, but before the economy crashed.

Independent clause:

A real estate market crash occurred in the city

Dependent clause:

After Léandre bought a penthouse,

Dependent clause:

but before the economy crashed.

Your Sentence

Relative Clauses (Defining and Non-Defining)

Inside complex sentences, you'll find another type of clause called a relative clause. There are two types of relative clauses, defining and non-defining.

Defining relative clauses

A defining relative clause is a clause that gives supplemental information about the subject of a sentence. Consider the following sentence, where relative clause is bolded.

Ex.: The real estate agent ***who helped Léandre buy the penthouse*** *was friendly and useful.*

Your Sentence

The sentence above contains a defining clause because we are not talking about any real estate agent, but the specific one who helped Léandre. It is part of the subject.

Non-Defining Relative Clauses

A non-defining relative clause is a clause that gives supplemental information about the subject of a sentence. Consider the following sentence, where the non-defining relative clause is bolded.

Ex.: The real estate agent, ***who helped Léandre buy the penthouse****, was friendly and useful.*

Your Sentence

____

____

This sentence contains a **non-defining clause** because we are presenting adding a <u>non-essential detail</u> to the sentence, namely, that the real estate agent helped Léandre buy the penthouse. For that reason, the clause is set off between two **commas**.

Defining clauses can be removed from the sentence without making them ungrammatical, but removing them will take away a detail that may be relevant to understand the sentence. In this case, we would not in which context the real estate was friendly and useful.

Correct Usage of Relative Clauses

Correct usage of **defining** and **non-defining clauses** is crucial because an error can change the meaning of a sentence. Consider, for example, the following two sentences:

Ex.: The New York City real estate agents ***who helped Léandre buy a property*** *have something in common.*

Ex.: The New York City real estate agents, ***who helped Léandre buy a property****, have something in common.*

The second sentence uses a non-defining relative clause that makes the sentence illogical. After all, it is impossible for all of New York City's real estate agents to have helped Léandre buy a property.

However, using a defining clause, as in the first sentence, makes logical sense. Here are some relative pronouns you can use in your relative clauses:

That	Who
Which	Whom
Whichever	Whose

Ex.: The properties ***that Léandre buy*** *have something in common.*

Your Sentence

____

____

Ex.: Léandre, ***whose penthouse is being renovated****, is gone on a vacation.*

Your Sentence

____

____

Ex.: The properties ***which Léandre buy*** *have something in common.*

Your Sentence

____

____

Now that you've learned about the complex sentence and its two different types (loose and periodic), you are ready to learn about the compound sentence!

Lesson 12

A Compound Sentence Has Two Independent Clauses

***A* compound sentence *is made of at least two* independent clauses.**

You can compound your dream by adding independent variables.

If you add independent variables to your dream, your dream compounds and becomes bigger. More variables means more complexity. This is inevitable when you follow your dreams. As you reach toward your goals, you set new targets and strive to go higher. The same is true in writing: The independent variables compound one another, which results in more information being conveyed in the sentence.

In this lesson, you will

- Learn what a **compound sentence** is
- See a list of **conjunctions** you can use to create compound sentences

A **compound sentence** is made of at least two **independent clauses**. The independent clauses must be separated either by a **comma + a coordinating conjunction** or by a semicolon (;).

Compound sentences contain more than one idea. Every independent idea represents one idea. A **compound sentence** could be two sentences.

When you choose to use the **semicolon** (;) to separate two **independent clauses**, the connection between the two **clauses** is not as clear—and it will be up to the reader to decide what the connection is. However, using the **semicolon** can vary your writing and improve your style.

The meaning of your **compound sentence** changes based on the connection between the two ideas. Such meaning is based on the connector you decide to use, namely, a **coordinating conjunction** or a **semicolon**. Each coordinating conjunction has a different meaning.

The **semicolon**, on the other hand, does not have an obvious meaning. When you use it, the reader has to figure out the connection between the two ideas. Although the **semicolon** can vary your style, you may not use it as often as **coordinating conjunctions** as it is more ambiguous. More on this in the next lesson.

Short list of coordinating conjunctions:

Coordinating Conjunction	Meaning
For	Because
And	Adding something
Nor	Negating something
But	Contradicting something
Or	Adding an option
Yet	Stronger contradiction than "but"
Since	Period of time **or** "because"

You can also use "because" as a **subordinating conjunction**, but you don't need to put a comma in front of it. (More on this in part 4). Instead of a **comma** and a **subordinating conjunction**, you can also use a **semicolon** (;) to separate two **independent clauses.** Moreover, the conjunction "for" and "since," don't need commas when they mean "because."

Ex.: Léandre bought the penthouse for his heart told him to.

Independent clause:

Léandre bought the penthouse

Dependent clause:

for his heart told him to.

Your Sentence

____

____

Ex.: Léandre bought the penthouse, and he said he loves it.

Independent clause:

Léandre bought the penthouse,

Independent clause:

and he said he loves it.

Your Sentence

____

____

Ex.: Léandre wasn't happy about the price, nor was he excited.

Independent clause:

Léandre wasn't happy about the price,

Independent clause:

nor was he excited.

Your Sentence

____

____

Note that the coordination conjunction requires to reverse the pronoun (he) and the verb (was).

Ex.: Léandre bought the penthouse, but it was overpriced.

Independent clause:

Léandre bought the penthouse,

Independent clause:

but it was overpriced.

Your Sentence

____

____

Ex.: Léandre bought the penthouse, or he would not have moved.

Independent clause:

Léandre bought the penthouse,

Independent clause:

or he would not have moved.

Your Sentence

____

____

Ex.: Léandre bought the penthouse, yet he is still looking.

Independent clause:

Léandre bought the penthouse,

Independent clause:

yet he is still looking.

Your Sentence

____

____

Ex.: Léandre bought the penthouse since it was his favorite.

Independent clause:

Léandre bought the penthouse

Independent clause:

since it was his favorite.

Your Sentence

____

____

Ex.: Léandre bought the penthouse; it was his favorite.

Independent clause:

Léandre bought the penthouse;

Independent clause:

it was his favorite.

Your Sentence

____

____

Now that you've learned about the compound sentence, you are ready to learn about the last and most complex type of sentence—the compound-complex sentence!

Lesson 13

A Compound-Complex Sentence Has Two Independent Clauses and at Least One Dependent Clause

***A compound-complex sentence consists of* two sentences*, one of which must be a* complex sentence.**

You can make your dream more complex or compound it, but you can also do both.

You can add dependent variables to your dream, which makes it complex. You can also add independent variables, which makes it compound. But you can do both things at once, which makes your dream both complex and compounded. The same is true of the last sentence type, the **compound-complex sentence**.

In this lesson, you will

- Learn what a **compound-complex sentence** is
- When it is appropriate to use **compound-complex sentences**

A **compound-complex sentence** is made of at least two **independent clauses** and at least one **dependent clause**. In other words, it consists of **two sentences**, one of which must be a **complex sentence**. Compound-complex sentences are not very common today, and you should use them with caution. It's typically best to write simple and complex sentences, but some situations call for compound-complex sentences (when the ideas are particularly complicated).

Ex.: Before he bought the penthouse, Léandre shopped around the city, and he made several offers.

Dependent clause:

Before he bought the penthouse,

Independent clause:

Léandre shopped around the city,

Independent clause:

and he made several offers.

Your Sentence

____

____

Ex.: Before he bought the penthouse, Léandre shopped around the city; he made several offers.

Dependent clause:

Before he bought the penthouse,

Independent clause:

Léandre shopped around the city;

Independent clause:

he made several offers.

Your Sentence

____

____

Ex.: Léandre made several offers, but he had a great price because he was persistent.

Independent clause:

Léandre made several offers,

Independent clause:

but he had a great price

Dependent clause:

because he was persistent.

Your Sentence

____

____

Ex.: After Léandre bought a penthouse, but before the economy crashed, a real estate market crash occurred in the city.

Dependent clause:

After Léandre bought a penthouse,

Dependent clause:

but before the economy crashed,

Independent clause:

a real estate market crash occurred in the city.

Your Sentence

____

____

By now, you've explored all the different types of sentences. To create these sentences, we need to use specific punctuation marks. In the next section, you will learn how to use these punctuation marks.

Now that you have learned the fundamentals of sentence structure—including parts of speech, word roles, phrases, and clauses—you know how to build sentences clearly and effectively. But to make sure your sentences are precise and accurate, you need to use proper punctuation. Without proper punctuation, your message might confuse your reader.

Part IV

Basic Punctuation

Lesson 14

Punctuation Shows Relationships Between Words and Sentences

Punctuation gives meaning to our sentences by indicating the relationship between different layers of your text.

You'll take pauses between the different parts of your dream.

Punctuation is simple and complicated at once. It can seem unimportant, but it is vital to your writing. According to the Oxford Dictionary, punctuation "is the practice, action, or system of inserting points or other small marks into texts in order to aid interpretation; division of text into sentences, clauses, etc., by means of such marks."

Punctuation gives meaning to sentences by indicating the relationship between different components of your text (clauses, phrases, word roles, and parts of speech). Without punctuation, it is virtually impossible to read a text. Poor punctuation leads to poor representation of ideas. Plus, as we will see in Part 5, punctuation is critical in creating your writing style.

In this part of the book, we will go over all **punctuation signs** with some examples. Unlike in the previous lessons, where we dealt with sentence structure, this lesson does not analyze every sentence with all its components. By now, these components should be clear.

Before getting into punctuation, let's address **capital letters**. In the English language, capital letters are not used very often, and overusing capital letters can hinder your credibility. We use capital letters when beginning sentences, for proper nouns, and for the pronoun "I".

Using capital letters in contexts other than the conventional ones places emphasis on the word capitalized. While in some cases that may be fine, in some other it may look overly grandiose and pompous. For example, take the sentence "I like Money, Fame, and Status."

Conventions say you shouldn't capitalize the words money, fame, and status. Of course, you're free to do so if you want. But you should be aware that many readers will see this as bizarrely extravagant. Earlier in history, we used to capitalize important words, and the German language still does today. But we are in the twenty-first century, and the language we are dealing with is English, not German. Note that there are some exceptions, as in legal writing. In any case, you should use judgment and discernment.

Lesson 15

Periods (.) End Sentences and Ellipses (...) Show Omission

Whether you are dealing with a simple, complex, compound, or compound-complex sentence... you are going to use either the period (.) to end the sentence neutrally or with an ellipsis (...) to show that you are omitting information.

Some pauses show the end of something neutrally and others with omissions.

What's the difference between the end of a movie and the end of a TV show episode? Typically, a movie ends after the resolution of the **intrigue**. Unless the movie is part of a series, there's nothing left to resolve after the end. A TV show episode, however, never ends with everything solved – except for final episodes. Instead, it omits necessary information to create a sense of intrigue and pushes you to watch the next episode. The same is true of periods (.) and ellipses (...)

Most sentences are what we call "declarative sentences." The only sentences that are not declarative are those with exclamation marks and question marks, which we will see in the next few sections. Whether you are dealing with a simple, complex, compound, or compound-complex sentence, you are likely dealing with a declarative sentence. In those cases, you are going to use either the period (.) to end the sentence neutrally or with an ellipsis (…) to show that you are omitting information.

Period in Sentences

Ex.: Léandre bought the penthouse.

Your Sentence

Ex.: After talking to the real estate agent, Léandre bought the penthouse.

Your Sentence

Ex.: Léandre bought the penthouse, and he felt content.

Your Sentence

Ex.: After talking to the real estate agent, Léandre bought the penthouse, and he felt content.

Your Sentence

Ellipsis in Sentences

When you use an ellipsis in a sentence, you are indicating that you are leaving information out, which creates a sense of intrigue. Be careful not to overuse the ellipsis as your reader will start to find it meaningless.

Ex.: Léandre bought the penthouse…

Your Sentence

____

____

Now that you know how to end sentences with and without omission, you need to learn how to end sentences with intense emotions. To this we will turn in the next lesson.

Lesson 16

Exclamation Marks (!) Intensify Emotions

Some sentences show strong emotions, and to show strong emotions, you can use the exclamation mark.

Some parts of your dream will be more intense than others.

As you move toward your dream, you will inevitably feel **strong emotions** from time to time. Any dream worth achieving comes with a roller coaster of emotions. The same is true in writing: Some sentences show strong emotions, and to show strong emotions, you can use the exclamation mark. But be careful: overusing the exclamation mark backfires against the writer. Like with the ellipsis, you will make your exclamation marks meaningless if you use them too often.

You should use the exclamation mark moderately, and you should make sure you are not using it when the strong emotion (e.g., anger, shock, surprise) are not already made obvious by the words. Misusing the exclamation mark will show contempt and disregard for your reader. Above all, never, ever use more than one exclamation mark. Doing so tells your reader that you believe they are incapable of grasping the significance of what you are saying. Should that be the case, then you are at fault — not the reader.

You can use the exclamation mark at the end of a sentence to show emotions. This turns your declarative sentence into an exclamative sentence. Remember that, as a rule of thumb, most of your sentences should be declarative.

Ex.: Léandre bought the penthouse!

Your Sentence

____

____

Now that you've learned how to end sentences with intense emotions, you need to learn how to end sentences when they are questions. To this we turn in the next lesson.

Lesson 17

Question Marks (?) Cause Direct Questions

Every sentence you write or speak provides information which answers questions—even if the question wasn't stated. But in some cases, you must be the one asking the questions—directly.

Some parts of your dream will leave you with questions.

Writing is always about **answering questions**. Every sentence you write or speak provides information which answers questions—even if the question wasn't stated. But in some cases, you must be the one asking the questions—directly. In those cases, the roles are reversed. You are not responding, but you are asking. To ask direction questions, we use the question mark (?). Direct questions are made with sentences where the **subject** and the **verb** are reversed ("are you" VS. "you are").

When you reverse the **subject** and the **verb**, you must consider the auxiliary and the verb tense. The auxiliary is a second verb that helps your main verb (e.g., be, do, have). The verb tense is the time when the action is being done (e.g., past, present, future.)

Ex.: Did Léandre buy the penthouse?

Your Sentence

____

____

Ex.: Will Léandre buy the penthouse?

Your Sentence

____

____

Ex.: Does Léandre buy the penthouse?

Your Sentence

____

____

Ex.: Has Léandre bought the penthouse?

Your Sentence

____

____

By reversing the subject and the verb, and by adding a question mark, you are making sentences **interrogative sentences**—instead of **declarative**. Again, most of your sentences should be declarative.

Don't use question marks for indirect questions such as, "The real estate agent asked Léandre if he felt good when they proceeded to the transaction." The latter sentence is a **declarative sentence**.

Now that you've learned how to end sentences in the different ways, let's turn to punctuation marks that connect words. To these we turn in the next few lessons.

Lesson 18

Hyphens (-) Separate Words

Hyphens connect words in a way that creates meaning from different words. In a sense, they compound words together.

Some parts of your dream stick together to make sense.

Sometimes, meaning is created not just by one word, but by two or more words. Hyphens connect words in a way that creates meaning from different words. In a sense, hyphens compound words together. That said, not all compound words use a hyphen, and this can lead to confusion. There is no precise rule that stipulates which nouns and verbs use a hyphen. When in doubt, use a dictionary.

It's easy to find out if compound **nouns** and **verbs** use hyphens by looking in a dictionary. For example, "printing press," "car wash," and "chief of staff" don't use a hyphen, while "eye-opener," "check-in," and "free-for-all" do. The same thing goes for verbs, where "waterproof" and "highlight" don't use a hyphen, while "rubber-stamp" and "nickel-and-dime" do.

As far as adjectives go, you won't find out in the dictionary whether you should use a hyphen or not. To understand whether or not you need to hyphenate a compound adjective, you need to understand if the two or more words collectively act as an adjective. If so, then you need to hyphenate these words.

*Ex.: The real estate agent was a **do-nothing**.*

Your Sentence

____

____

*Ex.: The real estate agent used **state-of-the-art** negotiation techniques.*

Your Sentence

____

____

Now that you've learned when and how to use the hyphen to connect words, you need to learn another way of connecting words—apostrophes.

Lesson 19

Apostrophes (') Show Possession Between Nouns

***What's interesting about nouns is that they can belong to another noun. For example, an animal, a plant, or an object can belong to a person. In those cases, we are talking about* possession.**

Some parts of your dream belong to another.

We use **nouns** to identify people, animals, plants, objects, places, etc. What's interesting about nouns, though, is that they can belong to another noun. For example, an animal, a plant, or an object can belong to a person. In those cases, we are talking about **possession** because one noun possesses another. To indicate possession, we use **apostrophes**.

While **nouns** can be accompanied by an adjective, it is still to the nouns that the apostrophe is connected. Remember that **nouns** are parts of speech, but that a **part of speech** is not necessarily enough to create the subject in a sentence. In some cases, we need more information, which leads us to make a phrase—a noun phrase, specifically.

Ex.: Léandre's penthouse is located in New York City.

Your Sentence

____

____

Ex.: The penthouse's patio overlooks New York City's skyline.

Your Sentence

____

____

Ex.: Léandre's girlfriend wanted to buy the penthouse

Your Sentence

____

____

Now that you know how to connect a noun that belongs to anther with apostrophes, you need to learn another punctuation mark similar to the apostrophe—the quotation marks.

Lesson 20

Quotation Marks ("quote") Show Citation and Dialogue

We call the attribution of text to a person* ci-tation*. Citing is common in all types of text ranging from academic writing to novels.

Conversations occur as part of your dream.

While some nouns belong to other nouns, some text passages can belong to people. We call the attribution of text to a person **citation**. Citing is common in all types of text ranging from academic writing to novels. For example, in academic papers, we cite other authors' works to enrich our own work. In novels, we include **dialogue** between characters to drive the action and showcase the characters. We also refer to citing as "quotations."

There are two types of quotations—**direct** and **indirect**. We use direct quotation to cite someone else's words exactly how they were spoken or written. Direct quotation requires us to use quotation marks, which is what this lesson is about. Indirect quotation, however, is when we refer to what someone has said or written but have rephrased in our own words. Indirect quotation does not require us to use quotation marks. Note that in either case, you should be mentioning the author. To learn more about how to do so, consult the style guide used in your discipline or by your publisher.

Depending on what precedes or follows the quoted passage, you may have to use certain punctuation marks.

Quoted Passages Preceded by a Dependent Clause

When your quoted passage is introduced by an independent clause, put a comma before your quoted passage as with any dependent clause. We often use dependent clauses to introduce what other people have said.

Ex.: According to the journalist, ***"Léandre Larouche bought a penthouse in one of New York City's most expensive neighbhorhoods."***

Your Sentence

Ex.: As Léandre told the journalist, ***"New York City is one of the world's greatest wonders."***

Your Sentence

Quoted Passages Preceded by an Independent Clause

When your quoted passage is introduced by an independent clause, put a colon before the quoted passage. We often use an independent clause to introduce a quoted passage to give strength to the statement.

Ex.: The journalist reported: ***"Léandre Larouche bought a penthouse in one of New York City's most expensive neighbhorhoods."***

Your Sentence

Quoted Passages Preceded by the Word "That"

When you use the word "that" before your quoted passage, no punctuation mark is required. The word "that" connects the first part of your sentence with the quoted passage.

Ex.: The journalist reported that ***"Léandre Larouche bought a penthouse in one of New York City's most expensive neighbhorhoods."***

Your Sentence

Quoted Passages Followed by More Text

If your quoted passage is followed by more text, put a comma before closing the quotation. Often, we quote a passage before attributing it to a speaker.

Ex.: ***"New York City is one of the world's greatest wonders,"*** *Léandre told the journalist.*

Your Sentence

Ex.: ***"New York City,"*** *Léandre told the journalist,* ***"is one of the world's greatest wonders."***

Your Sentence

____

____

Ex.: When the journalist reported that ***"Léandre Larouche bought a penthouse in one of New York City's most expensive neighbhorhoods,"*** *the economy crashed.*

Your Sentence

____

____

In the United States, punctuation marks go inside quotation marks, as you've seen in the last examples. However, conventions vary from one country to another and between citation styles. Double check conventions by consulting your discipline's or your publisher's style guide.

Now that you've learned how to use basic punctuation marks, which connect words, you are ready to learn advanced punctuation marks, which connect phrases and clauses.

Part V

Advanced Punctuation

Lesson 21

Commas (,) Separate Dependent Clauses, Phrases, and Lists of Words

One of the first uses of the comma is to indicate short pauses in a sentence. The connection between words, phrases, and clauses is made clear by the use of clauses.

Your dream requires simple pauses.

The comma is a complex punctuation mark, and it confuses many users of the English language. The primary reason for such confusion is the existence of multiple different uses for the comma. Pay attention to the different ways in which the comma is used in this lesson.

One of the first uses of the comma is to indicate **short pauses** in a sentence. The connection between words, phrases, and clauses is made clear by the use of commas. Pay particular attention to how you use commas because they can change the meaning of your text significantly.

In this lesson, you will

- Learn how commas separate dependent from independent clauses
- Learn how commas separate nonessential phrases
- Learn how commas separate words in lists
- Learn how commas indicate important nuances

Commas Separate Dependent from Independent Clauses

In a complex sentence where the dependent clause comes before the independent clause—also known as a **periodic sentence**—use a comma to separate the dependent from the independent clause.

Ex.: After Léandre bought a penthouse in New York City, the economy crashed.

Your Sentence

____

____

A common mistake people make with the comma is using it to separate two **independent clauses**. For example, the sentence "Léandre bought a penthouse in New York City, the economy crashed." is incorrect. Separating two independent clauses with a comma is grammatically incorrect and can confuse readers about the connection between the two clauses.

Another common mistake is to separate two **contradictory clauses** (marked by the word "however") with a comma. For example, the sentence "Léandre bought a penthouse in New York City, however, he lives in Canada." is incorrect. The correct way to express this sentence is "Léandre bought a penthouse in New York City. However, he lives in Canada." Another correct way to express this sentence is: "Léandre bought a penthouse in New York City; however, he lives in Canada."

The more clauses you have in a sentence, the more complicated using commas get. However, there are some rules of thumb. Most tricky situations with commas occur when you have two or more independent clauses *and* a transition between them.

Ex.: Léandre bought a penthouse in New York City, but in the end, he didn't like it.

Your Sentence

____

____

The sentence above contains two **independent clauses** and one **prepositional phrase** (in the end) that acts as a transition. It represents how we typically punctuate this type of sentence. However, there are other ways to punctuate a sentence like this. One school of thought, which is no longer popular today, suggests you can write the sentence as follows:

Ex.: Léandre bought a penthouse in New York City, ***but, in the end****, he didn't like it.*

Your Sentence

____

____

Some people take issue with the previous sentence because it is <u>overly punctuated</u>. However, you are free to decide whether you want to use more or less punctuation in your writing style. A more popular option today is to use the natural inflection we would use when speaking and remove the comma before the conjunction.

Ex.: Léandre bought a penthouse in New York City ***but, in the end****, he didn't like it.*

Your Sentence

____

____

Commas Separate Nonessential Phrases

When your sentence contains a **nonessential phrase**, use a comma to separate the nonessential phrase from the rest of the sentence. These phrases can be noun phrases, verb phrases, prepositional phrases, or adverbial phrases.

*Ex.: **In 2030**, Léandre will buy a penthouse.*

Your Sentence

____

____

Ex.: **To treat himself**, *Léandre will buy a penthouse.*

Your Sentence

____

____

*Ex.: **Slowly but surely**, Léandre will buy a penthouse*

Your Sentence

____

____

*Ex.: **Tired of Toronto**, Léandre bought a penthouse in New York City.*

Your Sentence

____

____

Commas Separate Words in Lists

Commas separate words that are the same part of speech in a list. When you make lists in a sentence, always use the same **part of speech** or else your list will be confusing and may not make sense to your reader. Lists comprise three elements or more. If you only enumerate two elements, use the word "and" to separate these elements.

Not a List (So no comma)

Ex.: Léandre bought a penthouse and a house.

Your Sentence

When you list three elements or more, you have a stylistic choice to make. You can either place a comma before the word "and," which indicates the last element as the last in the list. Using such a comma is referred to as the "serial comma" or the "Oxford comma." Certain style guides use it, while others don't. The reason the serial comma is often used is that it can avoid confusions in sentences.

Sentence Without the Oxford Comma

Ex.: Léandre bought a penthouse, ***a car and a house****.*

Your Sentence

Sentence With the Oxford Comma

Ex.: Léandre bought ***a penthouse, a car, a horse and a carriage, and a house****.*

Your Sentence

Commas Indicate Important Nuances

Commas are used in many other different contexts to indicate **small nuances**. Such contexts include numbers, dates, degrees and certifications, direct address, and geographic references.

When writing numbers, use a comma after the first digit of a four-digit number, the second digit of a five-digit number, and the third digit of a six-digit number. Numbers that have seven digits or more require more commas.

Ex.: Léandre spent ***$4,706*** *upfront to the real estate agent.*

Your Sentence

___

___

Ex.: Léandre spent ***$11,845*** *on travelling expenses.*

Your Sentence

___

___

Ex.: Léandre paid ***$11,845*** *in taxes.*

Your Sentence

___

___

Ex.: Léandre paid ***$4,076,500*** *for the penthouse.*

Your Sentence

___

___

*Ex.: Léandre paid **$4,834,760,000** for the skyscraper.*

Your Sentence

____

____

When writing about money, you may have to write a precise amount, including cents. When you need to write cents, use the period to separate dollars from cents.

*Ex.: Léandre paid **$11,845.92** in taxes.*

Your Sentence

____

____

When writing dates, use the comma to separate elements except the month and the day.

*Ex.: Léandre signed the paperwork on **Tuesday, April 7, 2030,** at 3:44 p.m.*

Your Sentence

____

____

When writing degrees and certifications, set off the degree or certification from the person's name with a comma.

*Ex.: Léandre Larouche**, B.A.,** signed the paperwork.*

Your Sentence

____

____

When addressing someone directly in writing, set off the person's name from the statement with a comma.

Ex.: "Thank you, ***Your Honor,****" said Léandre*

Your Sentence

When writing geographic references, use the comma to separate different elements.

Ex.: Léandre bought a penthouse in New York, ***NY.***

Your Sentence

Ex.: Léandre lives in ***New York, NY, USA,*** *and* ***Toronto, Ontario, Canada.***

Your Sentence

Now that you've learned the different uses of the comma, one of the most common punctuation marks, you are ready to learn how to use the semicolon, which is lesson common.

Lesson 22

Semicolons (;) Separate Independent Clauses and Complex Lists

Think of semicolons as complex pauses. They act like commas, but they are more nuanced because the connection they create is not as obvious.

Your dream requires complex pauses.

Unlike the comma, which can list parts of speech and separate dependent clauses from independent clauses, semicolons only separate **independent clauses**. They can separate different groups of elements that already contain commas.

Think of semicolons as complex pauses. They act like commas, but they are more nuanced because the connection they create is not as obvious. When you use a comma, you must use words that make the connection between words. It is not so with the semicolon. When you separate two independent clauses with a **semicolon**, you indicate the two clauses are **connected**, but you are not saying exactly how.

Ex.: Léandre bought a New York City penthouse; he is happy.

Your Sentence

____

____

If it weren't for the semicolon, the previous sentence would probably read something like "Léandre bought a New York City penthouse, and this purchase made him happy.

Semicolons also separate lists that have **complex elements** and that already contain commas or phrases. Each phrase acts like an item on the list. In other words, semicolons are used in lists when commas cannot.

Ex.: Léandre bought a penthouse in ***New York, NY; a house in Atlantic City, NJ; a mansion in Malibu, CA; and a town house in Kelowna, B.C.***

Your Sentence

____

____

Ex.: Léandre is friends with ***Scott, the philosopher; Matthew, the theologist; Cierra, the consultant; Bijal, the strategist; Carlos, the economist; Daniel, the poet; Richard, the professor; and Aaron, the cowboy.***

Your Sentence

____

____

Now that you know how to use commas and semicolons to create pauses in your writing, you are ready to learn about how colons introduce new elements.

Lesson 23

Colons (:) Introduce New Explanatory Clauses or Lists

Colons create a very clear connection between the elements they separate. Colons indicate that the first element causes the other following on.

Some parts of your dream are introduced by a previous event.

Colons are similar to semicolons, which is why they have a similar name. But unlike semicolons, colons create a very **clear connection** between the elements they separate. Colons indicate that the first element causes the following one(s). In other words, what comes after the colon is a product of what comes before the colon.

There are three main ways of using colons. The first one is to introduce a <u>new clause</u>, a <u>word</u>, a <u>phrase</u>, a <u>quotation</u>, an <u>example</u>, or an <u>explanation</u>. This use of the colon should be kept for rare occasion as it makes your writing choppy. The second use of the colon is to introduce a list. In the lesson on commas, we've talked about how to separate words in a list. In some cases, your list will naturally join the rest of your sentence. But in other cases, your list has to be introduced by a colon.

Ex.: Léandre bought a penthouse in one of New York City's best locations: ***the Upper East Side.***

Your Sentence

Ex.: Léandre made several purchases: ***a penthouse, a car, a mansion, and a town house.***

Your Sentence

Ex.: Léandre made the following statement: ***"I love New York City."***

Your Sentence

Ex.: The real estate agent said it the best: ***"This is New York City at its finest."***

Your Sentence

Ex.: Léandre is interested in three topics: ***politics, philosophy, and personal development.***

Your Sentence

Ex.: Léandre is an interesting character: ***half educator, half entertainer.***

Your Sentence

Now that you've learned how to introduce new elements, you are ready to learn how to connect and disconnect parts of your sentences with dashes.

Lesson 24

En Dashes (–) Show Relationships and Em Dashes (—) Break a Sentence's Flow

The en dash indicates opponents in a conflict or closeness in relationship. The em dash... can be used to break the sentence to include nonessential information.

Your dream gets connected and disconnected by events.

By now, we've looked at different ways of connecting parts of sentences. For example, we've seen how hyphen connect words and how commas connect phrases and clauses. There is an additional punctuation mark that **creates connections**, the en dash (–) and one that **shows a disconnection**, the em dash (—).

The en dash is <u>longer</u> than the hyphen but <u>shorter</u> than the em dash. The en dash indicates opponents in a **conflict** or **closeness** in relationship. How you type an en dash depends on your computer and keyboard. Some websites will tell you which keys to use to type an en dash based on your computer and keyboard. Google it!

Ex.: Léandre sides with Toronto in the ***New York–Toronto*** *debate.*

Your Sentence

____

____

Ex.: Léandre will move to New York City in ***2030-2031****.*

Your Sentence

____

____

The em dash, which is longer than the en dash, can be used to break the sentence to include **nonessential information** or to create a break in a sentence to produce an unexpected effect.

Ex.: Léandre—***who loves cosmopolitan cities***—*decided to move to New York City*

Your Sentence

____

____

Ex.: Léandre loves spending time in New York City—***alone.***

Your Sentence

____

____

Ex.: Léandre loves spending time in New York City—***or, rather, he likes walking down its streets.***

Your Sentence

____

____

Ex.: Léandre—***and all of his friends***—*love New York City.*

Your Sentence

____

____

Now that you've learned how to break a sentence's flow with the **en and em dashes**, you are ready to learn about adding supplementary information to your sentences with parentheses.

Lesson 25

Parentheses ( ) Disclose Non-Essential Information

When we use parentheses, we indicate to the reader that the information we provide is useful to what was previously said, but that ultimately, it is not as important and could be omitted.

Your dream sometimes contains unnecessary information.

Parentheses quite simply add **nonessential information** to sentences. The nonessential information can come in the form of a word, a phrase, a sentence, or multiple sentences. When we use parentheses, we indicate to the reader that the information we provide is useful to what was previously said, but that ultimately, it is not as important and could be omitted.

It's important to understand that when we write, we often add information that's not crucially important, but that is still helpful. Writing concisely and getting to the point fast is important, but details often contain richness we shouldn't withhold.

Ex.: Léandre **(*a man*)** *bought a penthouse in New York City.*

Your Sentence

____

____

Ex.: Léandre ***(and his girlfriend)*** *bought a penthouse in New York City.*

Your Sentence

____

____

Ex.: Léandre bought a penthouse in New York City. ***(He came close to forgetting about it.)***

Your Sentence

____

____

Ex.: Léandre bought a penthouse in New York City. ***(He had been wanting to do so for over a decade. It was one of his dreams.)***

Your Sentence

____

____

Now that you've learned about sentence structure and punctuation, you're ready to bring everything together and to learn how to write in the most effective way to your audience.

Part VI

Style and Audience Alignment

Lesson 26

Style is the Combination of All the Components of Grammar

Style is an art as much as a science because it not only allows you to show professionalism and a command of language, but it also allows you to distinguish yourself from others by showing your unique voice.

Your dream's style is made of its components.

Your dream consists of one action made in one place. But if that action was made by someone else, or in a different place, it would look completely different. That's **style**. You have your style, I have my style, and everyone else has their style. Our style is determined by the way we conduct ourselves. We may do the same things as other people, but we do them differently—with our style. The same is true in writing. We all use the same language and the same grammar, but we do it in different ways—according to our style.

Style is an art as much as a science because it not only allows you to show professionalism and a command of language, but it also allows you to distinguish yourself from others by showing your unique voice. Imagine driving a race car. To drive the car to your destination, you need to drive it appropriately, respecting the laws of physics, so that you avoid crashing it into a tree. As you drive the car, however, you want to make sure you are doing so with great style and gusto. You might accelerate and slow down, take long turns, slower ones, zigzag and show the vehicle's prowess. After all, you didn't get in the race car to look as though you are driving a Chevrolet, did you? Similarly, you didn't decide to write to be bland, boring, and unoriginal.

While style unfolds in two different fashions, it is always linked to the different elements of grammar and the levels of analysis. The first way in which style unfolds is appropriateness. Appropriateness refers to the correct usage of grammar. The second way in which style unfolds is originality. Originality refers to the fresh and unique usage of grammar to create engaging, recognizable text. In the end, you are always using grammar—but in different ways. Note these two ways are not mutually exclusive. Originality sometimes requires you to break the rules.

Lesson 27

You Can Write for a General, a Knowledgeable, or an Expert Audience

How much the person knows about your dream changes the conversation. You're going to talk about your dream in a different way depending on how much the person knows about it.

You can't talk about your dream to everybody the exact same way.

Before you talk to someone about your dream, you first need to know how much that person knows about your dream. Perhaps that person knows nothing about it. Perhaps that person knows a little. But perhaps that person knows everything possible about your possible. How much the person knows about your dream changes the conversation. You're going to talk about your dream in a different way depending on how much the person knows about it. There are indeed three types of audiences you can talk to:

1. **General audience**: the audience that knows little to nothing about your topic

2. **Knowledgeable audience**: the audience that knows some things about your topic
3. **Expert audience**: the audience that knows almost everything about your topic

It's generally easy to tell which audience you are talking to. If you can't make up your mind about which audience you're talking to, you risk confusing everyone. Experts on a topic don't want to read a general book on it. Likewise, the general audience doesn't want to read an expert book because it's too hard to understand.

After you've considered which of these audiences you are talking to, you need to consider the level of education of your target reader. Education is a crucial element as it indicates to you exactly how to write—especially as it relates to sentences. Ignoring your audience's level of education can once again put you at risk of confusing your audience—or, worse, sound condescending to them.

If your target readers are **college graduates** or have a **graduate degree**, they can easily read long sentences that have more than one idea. That's not a problem. However, do not make the mistake of sacrificing the readability of your text. If your target readers have a college degree or less, they may be able to read some long sentences, but they cannot sustain reading an entire work with long sentences comprised of many ideas.

If your target readers have a **high school** education only, they are unlikely to be able to read long, complicated sentences. While some may, many others may not. Your sentence length baseline should always be **15 to 20 words**. The more educated your audience is, the more freedom you have when it comes to writing longer sentences. Remember, however, that the further you go from 15 to 20 words, the more difficult it is to understand your text.

In the next paragraphs, you'll learn how to write to three different types of audiences. You'll also get real examples from my own writing life.

Writing for a General Audience

If you are writing for a general audience, you are writing for people who know little to nothing about your field and who may have little to no formal education. The goal of writing for a general audience is to reach as many people as possible. While people with a doctorate degree may be in your general audience, assume that your audience has as little education as possible.

To make sure your writing is understandable to the general audience, make sure you are writing **simple sentences**. You can use compound sentences and complex sentences as well, but avoid compound-complex sentences. When writing for a general audience, strive for short sentences. The average **plain sentence** in the English language comprises one idea and **15 to 20 words**.

While members of the general audience may be highly educated, others may not. Think about whether you are willing to sacrifice less educated readers to write longer, more **complex sentences**. The more ideas you put in a sentence, the more difficult it is to understand. The more words you put in a sentence, the more difficult it is to understand. 200 years ago, sentences were about 70-words long. Today, 70 words is by all standards inappropriate and unnecessarily difficult. 40 words is about as long as most sentences should be for a general audience.

As far as words go, **the longe**r they are, **the more difficult** they are to understand. If you are writing for a general audience, you should use simple words whenever you can. Words with one syllable are the shortest and the easiest to understand. **The more syllables** a word has, **the more obscure** the word might be for the audience. Avoid using words that have three, four, or more syllables unless you cannot find a simpler word. English takes its roots in both the Germanic and the Latinate languages. Germanic words tend to be simple and short while Latinate words tend to be long and complex. Readers with little education will stumble on Latinate words. If your readers have little education, avoid Latinate words as much as you can.

This is a list of Latinate words with their Germanic equivalent:

Latinate words	Germanic words
Assist (verb)	Help (verb)
Proceed (verb)	Go on (verb)
Beneficial (adjective)	Useful (adjective)
Abundant (adjective)	Many (adjective)
Intend (verb)	Mean (verb)
Furnace (noun)	Oven (noun)
Perceive (verb)	See (verb)
Grief (noun)	Sorrow (noun)
Comprehend (verb)	Understand (verb)
Observe (verb)	Watch (verb)
Mundane (adjective)	Worldly (adjective)
Lament (verb)	Weep (verb)
Occidental (adjective)	Western (adjective)
Annual (adjective)	Yearly (Adjective)

When writing for a **general audience**, you should also avoid any words specific to your field. While tempting, using words specific to your field will alienate your audience because they do not know what these words mean. When you choose words, ask yourself, are these words most people know and understand? If that's not the case, find a more common word or rephrase the sentence so that your meaning is clear. It's normal for readers to open the dictionary from time to time, but make sure they can understand at least 80% of the words.

Example of Writing for a General Audience

The following passage is an excerpt from "An American Dream Cut Short: Leaving the United States Amid the COVID-19 Crisis," which I published on the online platform Medium.com. I wrote it with a general audience in mind, namely, anyone interested in my adventures in the United States as a Canadian. I intended for anyone who is interested in education, travels, and politics to understand the article. That said, I assumed the audience would have a college education.

"After moving there in August 2019, I often thought there might have never been a better time for me to live in the United States. American politics fascinate me. Trump's impeachment by the House made me feel like I had a front seat before the stage of American history. Now, even though it saddened me to watch a country I admire tear itself apart, I couldn't help but feel an uncanny sense of intrigue and excitement. While the politics of drama unfolded at the White House, the politics of stopping Trump continued throughout the democratic primaries. Little did I know, these politics would be exacerbated and almost made to become trivial by the threat dawning upon us.

As early as the beginning of this year, the politics that fascinated me triggered the chaos in which we currently live. The Trump White House responded to the pandemic threat from China. That response was, to say the least, neither smooth nor swift. Politicians, experts, and the population couldn't agree about the threat's seriousness and the appropriate course of action. The coronavirus was disrupting our lives, and, as evident as it perhaps should have been, I cannot claim I saw it coming. What I can say, however, is that, on March 18, 2020, when I packed all my bags and rushed back to Canada in a rented car, there had never been and would never be a better time to leave the United States."

This article is an attempt to explain how it felt to be a Canadian in America at the time of COVID-19.

Write about your dream for a **general audience** (anybody):

____

____

____

____

____

Writing for a Knowledgeable Audience

If you are writing for a **knowledgeable audience**, you are writing for people who know some things about your field but who still have much to learn. The goal of writing for a knowledgeable audience is to write in such a way that is interesting for people familiar with your field but who don't know everything and may not have the highest level of education.

When writing for a knowledgeable audience, you have to ask yourself what is it that your audience takes for granted. You are responsible for determining what you assume and what you don't. Ultimately, however, your audience will be the judge of your work.

While you don't have to write overly **simple sentences** for a knowledgeable audience, you need to be careful that you are not packing too much information at once in your sentences. Doing so risks alienating your audience. A knowledgeable audience can contain people with **college degrees**, **graduate degrees**, and people with only **high school educations**. Write long, complicated sentences only if it's necessary to make your message clear. Ultimately, though, sentences have more to do with your target readers' education level than whether your audience is general, knowledgeable or expert. Make sure you know how educated your target reader is.

For a knowledgeable audience, you can use long, **multisyllabic words** — some being jargon — as long as they are part of the knowledge you are assuming your audience to have. Don't use complicated words simply because you want to. Be mindful of your audience.

Example of Writing for a Knowledgeable Audience

The following passage is an excerpt from "Multilingual Students and Tutors at the Concordia University's Writing Center" in the Dangling Modifier. I wrote this piece with a knowledgeable audience in mind, namely, fellow writing tutors. *The Dangling Modifier* is a peer-reviewed publication read mostly by writing tutors. Although knowledgeable about pedagogy, they are not experts as they are still pursuing their education. I intended for fellow writing tutors who share a common language (writing) to understand this piece.

"I set foot in Montreal's Concordia for the first time in January 2016. After moving from my small, French-speaking hometown in Canada, I started an undergraduate degree in English literature and professional writing. English was a challenge, as one would imagine, but the writing center proved a great resource from the start. For an ESL student who wrote every day, it was the perfect place: it was free, available, and effective. I went almost weekly and learned a great deal from the writing assistants. While I loved everything about it, there's one thing I loved more than the others: that the writing center eventually included me as part of its team even though I came to English late in my life. By the end of my first semester, I was hired as a writing assistant myself and would start working during the summer.

The writing center is a place where many students feel vulnerable. Non-native English speakers, most notably, can feel daunted and sometimes embarrassed. Many of them are great writers in their mother tongue, but writing in English can make them feel less articulate than they are. In his book *Multilingual Writers and Writing Centers*, Ben Rafoth (2015) writes, 'In most US writing centers, the assistance available for multilingual writers is not much different than it is for native speakers of English. Well intentioned and aware, writing center directors recognize multilingual writers need more assistance than most schools provide' (pp. 3-4). Rafoth (2015) then discusses Harris and Silva's position (1993), who argue that while tutors are better equipped to help native speakers, a few changes in tutoring style can greatly benefit non-native English speakers. Concordia University's writing center shows that hiring multilingual tutors when possible is an invaluable asset for the non-native English students.

It should be said that Concordia University is a place where a writing center can easily find multilingual tutors. It's a large, comprehensive university where English is the primary language of instruction; it's located in a multilingual city, in a predominantly French-speaking province, in an officially bilingual but mostly English-speaking country. The city of

Montreal is one of the most interesting case studies in Canadian diversity, with its multilingualism and its minority within a minority (English speakers in Québec). It should thus come as no surprise that Concordia's writing center, which serves students in English and French, is a place that strikes the imagination. Students and tutors speak different languages with beautiful accents while working on written works from a wide range of disciplines. It's impossible not to fall in love with the idea of the writing center at Concordia."

Write about your dream for a **knowledgeable audience** (people familiar with what the dream is about):

Writing for an Expert Audience

If you are writing for an **expert audience**, you are writing for people who know almost everything in your field. You should assume that they know everything about your field, except what is **novel** and unavailable to them (e.g., your own discoveries). Even if experts in your field don't know about something you're writing about, they will easily look it up. Unlike the general and knowledgeable audiences, the expert audience will eagerly search everything unknown.

Members of the expert audience are likely **well educated**—whether formally or informally. If they don't have degrees, they have read extensively and consumed information as well as applied it. As such, you do not need to worry too much about education.

You can write long, **difficult sentences** for an expert audience. Make sure, however, not to make your writing long and complicated for the sake of it. That would be a mistake. You should not sacrifice readability because you can afford to write long, complicated sentences. You shouldn't see this opportunity to show your literary superiority and engage in unwarranted writing extravaganza!

Experts too want to read clear, concise materials. They accept to read complicated materials when needed, but most do so out of necessity, not out of enjoyment. While some may enjoy complicated writing, do not assume these people constitute the majority. It would be a costly mistake to do so.

With an expert audience, you can use as many long, multisyllabic words as you want—and you can use all the jargon you please. However, do remember that being an expert does not mean you want boring, texts. They too want to read good stuff, which is what we discuss in the next lesson.

Example of Writing for an Expert Audience

The following passage is an excerpt from *The American Hyperbole After 2016: DeLillo's White Noise, Donald Trump, the Intellectual Dark Web and their Postmodern Paradigm* (my undergraduate thesis). I wrote this piece with an expert audience in mind, namely, my undergraduate thesis supervisor. I did not intend this piece to be understood by the general public. I intended for my undergraduate supervisor to understand my point and to demonstrate my understanding of the topic.

"One indicator of literary value is an author's ability to make incisive comments about the current state of a society while staying relevant as this very society evolves. In this department, authors of dystopian novels such as George Orwell tend to steal the spotlight as they deliberately write about the future, leaving more room for prescience. But other novels, even though less interested in what the future holds, succeed in remaining pertinent for decades due to their insights. Don DeLillo's *White Noise* is one of these novels. More than thirty years has passed since its publication, in 1986, and yet the novel only becomes more relevant. The 9/11 attacks, which occurred fifteen years after the publication of *White Noise*, as Jesse Kavadlo writes in 2004, made "belief, spirituality, and the possibility of redemption" more important to DeLillo's writing. "We are living in a Don DeLillo moment, to be sure," Kadavlo argues. "But we have occupied Don DeLillo's worlds for longer than just the last year, or decade, or even century" (Kadavlo 12). Kadavlo is correct in his assertions, even more so than he may have imagined when he made them. If the attacks on the World Trade Center changed the way we think of DeLillo's writing, so should what happened another fifteen years later: the rise of the Intellectual Dark Web (I.D.W.) and the election of Donald Trump as president of the United States of America. *White Noise* has become more relevant post-2016 than post-1986 or post-2001 because we now have a clear picture of what the United States has become under the predicament described by DeLillo. The novel's themes that may have looked like the products of their time (e.g., postmodernism, globalization, hyper consumption, and nuclear anxieties) have not faded away, but rather changed in shape. In fact, there has never been a better time to be reading *White Noise* than now. Not only can we better understand the issues the United States face in the post-2016 period through *White Noise*, including the buzzword postmodernism has become, but we can also shed a new light on DeLillo's widely commented upon work through the current American political context. But to do so requires zooming out from the America that DeLillo and some literary scholars describe and taking a broader perspective."

Write about your dream for an **expert audience** (people who know all about what your dream is about):

Now that you've learned about the three different types of audiences, you are well on your way to writing efficiently. However, there is another element you need to make sure you get right. That element is **tone**, and to this we turn in the next lesson.

Lesson 28

You Can Write in A Formal, Informal, or Neutral Tone

You can think of the tone as the mood or the vibe. Another way to think about it is location. For example, if you are having drinks at bar, you'll speak differently than if you're doing a job interview.

You can talk about your dream in different tones.

In writing, the audience is king, but context is prince. That is to say, you should figure out the audience you are writing for—general, knowledgeable, or expert—and then **the tone** that's more appropriate for the specific piece of writing. You can think of the tone as the mood or the vibe. Another way to think about it is location. For example, if you're having drinks at a bar, you'll speak differently than if you're doing a job interview. Similarly, you will likely speak to your colleagues differently than you speak to your parents.

In writing, the different tones—or contexts—are called **levels of formality.** They reflect the context in which we are writing. They are the writing equivalent of locations. The three levels of formality are:

1. **Formal**: formal is the *level of formality* we use when we need to be taken seriously and seem polite and professional. This level of formality is most appropriate with an expert audience.
2. **Informal**: informal is the *level of formality* we use when we don't need to be taken seriously and we can afford to look unprofessional. This level of formality is most appropriate for a general audience.
3. **Neutral**: neutral is the *level of formality* we use when being taken seriously does not matter, but the context isn't completely casual. This level of formality is most appropriate for a knowledgeable audience.

Writing With an Informal Style

An informal style means writing as though you were talking to your friend across the dinner table. It takes a personal tone, and it includes emotions. With an **informal style**, you can use the first-, second-, and third-person and you are likely to address the reader directly.

In informal writing, short sentences are acceptable. Syntax can be broken; for example, you can end a sentence with an ellipsis (...) and then add a fragment (non-complete sentence). Moreover, since an informal style means writing as though we are speaking, it means we should not craft complicated sentences with fancy combinations of clauses. When we speak, we typically use **loose sentences** (independent clause first and dependent clause last). We also use **periodic sentences** (dependent clause first and independent clause last), but not as often.

In informal writing, sentences tend to be shorter and less refined, which means we'll find less phrases. We won't find fancy series of phrases as in formal writing. The same is true of words, which are shorter and less sophisticated. In informal writing, contractions ("I'm" vs. "I am") and abbreviations ("TV" vs. "television" and "photos" vs. "photography") are acceptable.

Informal writing also tends to use a lot of **phrasal verbs**. Phrasal verbs are made of a verb and a preposition. Some examples include "take off," "blow up," "break down," "come forward," and "warm up." Phrasal verbs are rather informal, and they usually have a verb equivalent (e.g., take off vs. remove). **The more phrasal verbs** you use, **the more informal** your writing becomes. Colloquialisms and slang are also acceptable in informal writing — though it does not necessarily mean you should use them. The following passage is a short paragraph I wrote about a random topic. You'll see it written with an informal tone here and with other tones later.

"It was actually illegal in America to buy or produce alcohol for about a decade in the last century. The federal government banned alcohol because it needed to save grain for food during the first world war. But then Congress passed it as a regular bill. It was pretty hard to make sure people respect the law. Plus, it encouraged criminals to make money off illegal alcohol on the black market. In the end, alcohol was banned for 16 years, until Roosevelt changed the law because it wasn't good for the job market and the economy."

Write about your dream **informally:**

Writing With a Formal Style

In formal writing, you write as though you were talking to someone you must show respect to (e.g., the judge). Put otherwise, you are writing in a way that commands respect. Be as objective as possible. Formal writing is not personal and should contain a limited range of emotions and emotive punctuation (e.g., exclamation marks and ellipses). Avoid writing in the first- and second-person if you are using a formal writing style.

Short sentences are less acceptable in formal writing. At least, they should be used less often. Formal writing allows us to write long, complex sentences when warranted. It is well regarded and, depending on your audience, it can earn you respect. Formal writing also encourages the use of rhetorical decorations and an elaborate, sophisticated style.

Formal writing is unlike the way we speak — unless we are referring to a formal speech or address. Thus, we can play around with clauses and craft sentences with a number of combinations of clauses. **Periodic sentences** (dependent clause first and independent clause last) are preferable in formal writing. **Loose sentences** (independent clause first and dependent clause last) are not as much. Remember the 1:5 loose-to-periodic sentence ratio.

As far as words go, long and sophisticated words are acceptable in formal writing. Formal writing requires that words be as precise and resounding as possible. Additionally, contractions are not acceptable unless it's to make the text more readable. Abbreviations should be avoided. The following passage reuses the short paragraph from earlier and presents it in a formal style.

"From 1917 to 1933, the United States was in its period of prohibition, meaning that it was made illegal by the federal government to manufacture and sell alcoholic liquors. While the prohibition was initially implemented as a wartime measure due to a foreseeable shortage in grain, it was eventually passed as legislation by Congress as the 18th amendment. The prohibition was arduous to enforce, and it fostered illegal purchases. Although the legislation enjoyed broad support while it was in effect, President Franklin D. Roosevelt appealed it in 1933 to create jobs and generate revenue at the dawn of the Great Depression."

Write about your dream **formally:**

Writing With a Neutral Style

Writing in a **neutral style** is like talking to someone you just met. That said, we all have our different ways of talking to someone we just met. Some of us are more formal; some of us are more informal. Most of the time, you'll be writing with a neutral style. This means you'll be neither extremely formal nor informal. You'll be right in between, with elements of both. To find out how to write neutrally, revise the formal and informal styles as well as the different target audiences to create your neutral style. The following passage reuses the short paragraph from earlier and presents it in a neutral style—as *I* would write it.

"It used to be illegal in the United States to produce or purchase any type of liquor. The prohibition was first passed as a temporary measure during the first world war as a strategy to save grain that could be used on food production. Congress, however, eventually made it a bill. It was somewhat difficult to enforce the prohibition of alcohol, and it gave opportunities for criminals to profit on the black market. The ban lasted until 1933, when President Roosevelt decided to lift the ban because of the jobs and the money that was lost by such legislation."

Write about your dream **neutrally**:

Now that you've learned about the three different tones, it's time to make sure your writing is convincing. To be convincing, your writing needs to be clean and tight, which is what we cover in the next lesson.

Lesson 29

Convincing Writing is Tight

You should avoid any fluff or clutter that does not drive your point forward. In other words, you should be empathetic to your reader, who may not have a lot of time or attention.

You should waste no time when talking about your dream.

When talking to someone about your dream, you should assume that the person can get **uninterested** at any time. As a result, you should keep what you say about your dream short and concise. You should avoid any **unnecessary** words or sentences that don't drive your point forward. In other words, you should be **empathetic** to your reader, who may not have a lot of time or attention. By making your writing short and concise—tight, if you will—you are more convincing to your reader than if you don't because your reader will take your writing more seriously.

There are some timeless principles of compositions you should adopt to keep your writing tight and convincing. Some of these principles are famously mentioned in Strunk & White's *The Elements of Style*. Instead of attempting to reinvent the wheel, I have used and adapted some principles of composition from *The Elements of Style*, which is now in the public domain and can be downloaded for free online. This lesson is going to cover several of these composition principles.

Write Statements in the Positive Form

Unless you have an unavoidable reason to do so or are using irony, make definite assertions. Don't write statements in a negative form.

Léandre **did not** *think the price was* **unfair**.
VS.
Léandre thought the price was **fair**.

Léandre **was not** *challenged* **often**.
VS.
Léandre was **rarely** *challenged.*

Omit Needless Words

The most effective writing is concise and puts every word on trial for its life. Here are some examples from *The Elements of Style*:

the question as to whether	whether
there is no doubt but that	no doubt (doubtless)
used for fuel purposes	used for fuel
he is a man who	he
in a hasty manner	hastily
this is a subject which	this subject
His story is a strange one.	His story is strange.

Use Parallel Structures

In grammar, parallelism (or parallel structure) is a balance within one or more sentences of similar clauses or phrases that have the same structure. When you make a list, you need to make sure you use the same parts of speech across this list. Otherwise, your sentence is unparallel. Unparallel sentences are not only unpleasant to read, but they can also confuse your reader.

Unparallel nouns:
Léandre likes **drinking**, **eating**, and **to sleep**.

Parallel nouns:
Léandre likes **drinking**, **eating**, and **sleeping**.

Unparallel verbs:
Léandre likes **real estate** and **traveling**.

Parallel verbs:
Léandre likes **buying real estate** and **traveling**.

Parallel verbs alternative:
Léandre likes **to buy real estate** and **to travel**.

Unparallel prepositions:
Léandre ran **across** midtown, jumped **over** the fence, and **sprinted away**.

Parallel prepositions:
Léandre ran **across** midtown, jumped **over** the fence, and sprinted **down** the alley.

Examples of Parallelism in Rhetoric

Parallelism is not simply a requirement to write nice, grammatical sentences, but it is also a way to make your writing more convincing and more elegant. Rhetoric, or the art of persuasion, often uses parallelism to emphasize a point. Here are some famous examples:

"The inherent vice of capitalism is the unequal sharing of blessings. The inherent virtue of Socialism is the equal sharing of miseries."

— Winston Churchill, House of Commons, 22 October 1945.

"Let every nation know, whether it wishes us well or ill, that we shall pay any **price**, *bear any* **burden**, *meet any* **hardship**, *support any* **friend**, *oppose any* **foe** *to assure the survival and the success of liberty."*

— John F. Kennedy, Presidential Inaugural Address.

"... and that government **of** *the people,* **by** *the people,* **for** *the people, shall not perish from the earth."*

— Abraham Lincoln, Gettysburg Address.

"We have petitioned, and **our petitions** *have been scorned; we have entreated, and* **our entreaties** *have been disregarded; we have begged, and they have mocked when* **our calamity** *came. We beg* **no longer**; *we entreat* **no more**; *we petition* **no more**. *We defy them."*

— William Jennings Bryan, Cross of Gold.

Keep Related Words Together

Word order indicates the relationship between words. Words and groups of words related in thought must be **as close as possible**. Consider the following examples from *The Elements of Style*:

Incorrect

Ex.: Wordsworth, ***in the fifth book of The Excursion****, gives a minute description of this church.*

Correct

Ex.: ***In the fifth book of The Excursion****, Wordsworth gives a minute description of this church.*

Your Sentence

____

____

Incorrect

Ex.: Cast iron, ***when treated in a Bessemer converter****, is changed into steel.*

Correct

Ex.: ***By treatment in a Bessemer converter****, cast iron is changed into steel.*

Your Sentence

____

____

Stick to the Same Person and Tense Except When Warranted

Whether you are writing in the first-, second-, or third-person, stick to that person. To do so, think **linearly** when you write. Somebody is doing something at a certain point in time. Watch the **subject** you are using in any given paragraph. By keeping the subject consistent, it's easier to keep the verb tense the same because you have a clear map of where things are going. That said, you will sometimes need to change subject because something happen at different moments in time.

Keep the subject (the WHO) as consistent as possible. By doing so, you help your readers stay **focused** on the **information** you are presenting. Switching subjects too often shows the writer is <u>unfocused</u>. The best time to switch person or verb tense is when beginning a new paragraph. Consider the following example from a short story I've written:

"A small Midwestern town's mall stands for a lot more than stores gathered under one roof. It's even truer for you, who left this place several years ago, than it is for those who chose to stay and spend their lives here. The mall's the place you can go to when you're back, once in a while, but not too often, and decide to listen to your innate *voyeur*. The mall's the best place to contemplate the forever-gone reality of your childhood, the desolate world you've abandoned."

In the previous example, the subject consistently remains "the mall." The story is set in the present, but when I refer to the reader as "you," I occasionally use the past tenses because some actions were done in the past.

When writing about **facts** and **theories**, write in the **present tense**. When something has taken place in the past, write in the <u>past tense</u>. You may occasionally use the future tense when talking about the future. Make sure, however, that you avoid changing tense as much as possible. If you have a passage in the past, keep the past together. If you have information presented in the present tense, keep the present tense together.

When referring to other people's work, you need to distinguish between actions and discourses. Actions made in the past are written in the past tense. Consider the following sentence:

Ex.: Léandre ***bought*** *a penthouse in New York City.*

Discourse, however, requires the present tense. By discourse I mean what has been published in a work and will stand the test of time. When citing somebody else's work, you need to use the present time. Think about this way: writing lives forever but not actions. Consider the following sentence:

Ex.: Léandre Larouche ***writes****, in his book* The Architecture of Grammar, *that "Grammar is as much a code as mathematics."*

Your Sentence

Place the Emphatic Words at the End

Earlier in this book, we've talked about how information blocks come in order of important—the most important coming first and the least important block coming last. To this notion we need to add one nuance: **emphatic words** come at the end of a sentence. Words that give your sentence strength should come at the end because they are most memorable. See these examples from *The Elements of Style*:

Suboptimal

Ex.: Humanity has hardly ***advanced in fortitude*** *since that time, though it has advanced in many other ways.*

Optimal

Ex.: Humanity, since that time, has advanced in many other ways, but it has hardly ***advanced in fortitude****.*

Your Sentence

____

____

Suboptimal

Ex.: This steel is principally ***used for making razors****, because of its hardness.*

Optimal

Ex.: Because of its hardness, this steel is principally ***used in making razors****.*

Your Sentence

____

Don't Make Sentences Too Heavy with Verbs

Stacking verbs on top of one another and using too many passive or gerund (-ing) verbs make your writing heavier.

Suboptimal

*Ex.: **Charmed** by the neighborhood and being a lover of art, Léandre bought a penthouse in New York City, **adding** one more property to his portfolio.*

Optimal

*Ex.: **A lover of art and in love with the neighborhood,** Léandre bought a penthouse in New York City, **which added one more property to his portfolio**.*

Your Sentence

____

____

Use Signposting Language—Sparingly and Appropriately

Signposting language is the words and phrases used to make writing clear and easy to follow. We often use signposting language in public speaking, but we also use it in writing. Here are some examples of signposting:

Purpose	Signpost	Language
Introducing the topic	This book is about… By the end of this book, I	hope to have… Let us now look at...
Explaining the structure (sections / subtopics)	The first reason… The second reason…	The third reason… In the coming chapters...
Introducing the first section / subtopic, first of a list of points, or a story	Let's start by talking about... To begin,… Firstly,… I'll start with, …	he first advantage / reason / cause, etc. is… I'm going to tell you a story...
Finishing a section	We've looked at... I've talked about….	In this chapter, I considered… I have tried to...
Starting a new section	Let's move on to… Now, let's turn to… And I'd now like to talk about… The next / second …	Now let's look at... The next issue/topic/area...

Purpose	Signpost	Language
To signal the end of a chapter, section / Summing up	To sum up, … I have concluded, ... To recap, ... In sum, ... In conclusion, …	To summarize, … In summary, … Overall, … The three main points are

Now that you know how to make your writing clear and concise, you need to learn how to make your writing engaging. Although grammar helps you achieve clarity and conciseness in your writing, which is critical, it also helps make your writing engaging—which is just as important.

Lesson 30

Engaging Writing is Like a Good Thriller: It's Original and Has No Dull Moments

Your dream is yours—not your audience's. But you can make it compelling to your audience by making it original and interesting.

Your dream should be authentic and filled with interesting moments.

If you want to get someone to listen to you and pay attention, it's not enough to have a dream and **articulate** it. You need to express your dream in an **authentic** way—in a way only you can—and to make it so interesting your audience can't get enough of it. After all, your dream is yours—not your audience's. But you can make it compelling by making it original and interesting.

Throughout this book, we've mostly covered what is grammatically correct and what kind of writing is aligned with your audience. In this last lesson, we cover your **voice** and your **style**, which are the product of the different elements and patterns of grammar. You can name your writing if you wish. For example, I like to think of my writing style as "rogue" because I like to write punchy, playful, and witty texts. I do so by using grammar deliberately to create certain effects.

Remember that it's not easy to become an original writer and to have a recognizable voice. Moreover, your **originality** and **uniqueness** are a continuum. Your voice and style are not a yes-no type of thing. Finding your true **writing voice** will never be fully achieved as you'll always improve it. Your voice is an ideal you strive toward, not something you reach. As I write this book, I am still refining my writing style.

In this lesson, you will

- Learn how to use sentence length to your advantage
- Learn how clauses affect your writing style
- Learn how to leverage phrases to enrich your writing
- Learn the best types of words

Use Sentence Length to Your Advantage

Sentence length plays an important role in your writing style. While **short sentences** make your style punchier and more digestible, **long sentences** make your style refined, subtle, and sometimes more difficult. More difficulty isn't always a bad thing. Sometimes we need to stop and sniff the bouquet.

Speaking of length, note that what is true for sentences is also true for texts, chapters, and paragraphs. You can, for instance, vary the length of your chapters and paragraphs to keep your readers engaged. The shorter, the punchier — the longer, the more substantial.

When it comes to sentence types, which we have already covered, you should use all four of them. However, note that they give a different effect. I have listed below the four types of sentences in order of sophistication:

1 - **Simple Sentence** — contains only one idea and is short and punchy.

2 - **Complex Sentence** — contains only one idea, but it has another element that lengthens the sentence.

3 - **Compound Sentence** — contains two ideas as well as an addi-

tional element and can be rather long.

4 - **Compound-Complex Sentence** — contains two ideas and additional elements and is often quite long.

While you don't want to use **simple sentences** only, don't use too many **compound-complex sentences** either. Use each type, where appropriate, and make sure you find equilibrium. You will never have a perfect balance, namely, you will always lean toward simplicity or complexity, and this partly creates your style. For example, I tend to lean toward complexity more than simplicity.

Write a paragraph about your dream varying between all four types of sentences:

Clauses Affect Your Writing Style

Remember that, as you use sentences, you need to pay close attention to your clauses. As we covered earlier in the book, clauses make or break sentences. When it comes to style, it's important to emphasize the **loose-to-periodic** sentences ratio.

The types of clauses you use in sentences (*dependent* and *independent*) determine the types of sentences you are using. Remember that, if you want your writing to be solid, your **loose-to-periodic sentences** ratio should be about 1:5.

In other words, you should write approximately 1 sentence that finishes with a dependent clause (**loose**) for every 5 sentences that finish with an independent clause (**periodic**). This is just a rule of thumb, but make sure you do not overuse loose sentences.

That said, you can play around with clauses and see what kind of style you want to create. Through clauses, you build the **rhythm** of your text. To see how your writing sounds based on how you structure clauses, read your sentences out loud. Here is a paragraph with many loose sentences:

"The third concert of the subscription series was given last evening, and a large audience was in attendance. Mr. Edward Appleton was the soloist, and the Boston Symphony Orchestra furnished the instrumental music. The former showed himself to be an artist of first rank, while the latter proved itself fully deserving of its high reputation. The interest aroused by the series has been very gratifying to the Committee, and it is planned to give a similar series annually hereafter. The fourth concert will be given on Tuesday, May 10, when an equally attractive program will be presented."

Here is the same paragraph with a better loose-to-periodic sentences ratio:

"The third concert of the subscription series was given last evening. The concert was attended by a large audience. Mr. Edward Appleton was the soloist, supported by the Boston Symphony Orchestra on instruments. Mr. Edward Appleton showed himself to be an artist of first rank, at the same time, Boston Symphony Orchestra too proved itself deserving of its high reputation. Gratified by the interest shown, the Committee has planned to give a similar annual series hereafter. The fourth concert will be given on Tuesday, May 10, with an equally attractive program."

Write a paragraph about your dream with a good loose-to-periodic sentences ratio:

Leverage Phrases to Enrich Your Writing

Phrases are your chance to get creative. **Phrases** convey the information we need, such as WHO, WHAT, WHERE, WHEN, WHY, HOW, etc. As mentioned before, you always need a WHO and WHAT in a sentence. The rest is up to you.

It is in the rest that your creative potential lies. The WHEN, WHERE, WHY, HOW give you plenty of opportunities to make your writing savory. It allows you to be **descriptive**; it allows you to create metaphors and analogies; it allows you to create images in your readers' minds. The amount and type of information is what creates your style. Here are a few examples:

Imagery: Scenes set or items shown with descriptive words.

Ex.: When Léandre entered, the penthouse ***was deserted and spotless, the light shining on white immaculate walls.***

Your Sentence

____

____

Metaphor: a comparison that is not presented as a similarity but rather as a reality.

Ex.: The penthouse ***was a shining star*** *in the New York City market.*

Your Sentence

____

____

Ex.: The park below the penthouse ***is a mirror.***

Your Sentence

____

____

Ex.: High-rise buildings ***are flowers*** *in our cities.*

Your Sentence

Beyond these two examples, phrases that convey the WHO, WHAT, WHERE, WHEN, WHY, HOW, etc. give you the opportunity to create a voice, a mood, and a texture of your text by putting different words together. To do so, you must understand the power words have individually.

Furthermore, phrases allow you to lengthen and shorten your sentences. The amount of information you present in a sentence will determine the length of your sentences.

That said, you need to be mindful of only using phrases that **add genuine value to the sentence** and do not distract the reader from the topic and your text. Phrases such as "I believe" can be perceived as uncertain and take the reader's attention from your writing to you as a person. Consider the passage below:

"In every life, in every story, there is a theme, a statement, spoken not by the protagonist, but by an ally or an enemy. You can't overstate its importance. The statement represents a turning point, moral or intellectual, and it eventually comes back. By the end of the story, the protagonist becomes the higher of himself and reconsiders that statement in a new light."

This passage contains sentences that have multiple phrases, some of which repeat and emphasize certain elements. Each phrase adds value to the sentence it belongs to. You can have a lot of fun playing around with phrases and words. Make sure you understand punctuation deeply as it allows you to combine words and phrases correctly and beautifully.

Write a paragraph about your dream using phrases to create imagery and metaphors:

The words you choose for your writing are going to become a part of your **writer's identity**. Words can either make you strong or weak, so you must pick them carefully.

Words carry with them certain emotions through their connotation (which varies from one culture to the other), and together your words will give a certain energy (positive, negative, or otherwise) to your text. From a narrower standpoint, there are some best practices when using certain parts of speech.

Many of the words we use in sentences are words and nouns. There are weak nouns and strong nouns. There are also weak verbs and strong verbs. It's as simple and binary as that. It all depends on the context, but it's not confusing; there is no in between.

You know a noun is strong when you have a clear, unambiguous picture of what it is. The same goes for verbs. You have a strong verb when you have a clear, unambiguous picture of what the action is. Consider the follow sentences:

Weak

Ex.: Léandre and his friends ***walked*** *toward the building on a hot summer day.*

Stronger

Ex.: Léandre and his friends ***marched*** *toward the building.*

Your Sentence

____

____

Weak

Ex.: Léandre ***ran across*** *the street during the incident.*

Stronger

Ex.: Léandre ***sprinted across*** *the street during the incident.*

Your Sentence

____

____

When it comes to verbs, there are **three types** of verbs you want to avoid.

State-of-Being Verbs

State-of-being verbs are verbs that are passive instead of powerful. You should only use them when necessary as they make your writing weak. Here are some examples:

Is	Has	May
Am	Had	Might
Are	Do	Must
Was	Does	Can
Were	Did	Could
Be	Shall	Being
Will	Been	Should
Have	Would	

Weak

Ex.: Léandre ***is a lover*** *of art deco architecture.*

Stronger

Ex.: Léandre ***treasures*** *art deco architecture.*

Your Sentence

____

____

Weak

Ex.: Léandre ***was racing*** *by the park.*

Stronger

Ex.: Léandre ***raced*** *by the park.*

Your Sentence

____

____

Weak

Ex.: ***There are*** *three behaviors that make Léandre furious.*

Stronger

Ex.: ***Three behaviors*** *make Léandre furious.*

Your Sentence

____

____

Verbs That Rely on Adverbs

Verbs that require adverbs to convey meaning are not powerful enough. Powerful verbs are strong enough to stand alone. Here are some examples of verbs that rely on adverbs:

Walk	Run
Look	Any other ambiguous verb

Verbs That Finish with "-ing" Suffixes

Verbs with -ing suffixes, like passive verbs, make your writing heavier and more convoluted. Consider the following examples:

Weak

*He **was walking**.*

Stronger

*He **walked**.*

Your Sentence

Weak

*She **was loving** the food.*

Stronger

*She **loved** the food.*

Your Sentence

Weak

*They **were starting** to gather.*

Stronger

*They **started** to gather.*

Your Sentence

To recap, **adjectives and adverbs** are what happens when you use weak nouns and adverbs. Remember that adjectives modify nouns and adverbs modify verbs. You should use as few adjectives and adverbs as you possibly can.

When you use an adjective or an **adverb**, ask yourself, "could I find a noun/verb that makes it unnecessary to use an adjective/adverb?" First, to be certain, you want to look up the word in a thesaurus. Since every synonym has a slightly different meaning, you may not find the noun or verb you are looking for. If the answer can replace your noun or verb, do it. If you can't replace it, don't. Stephen King famously said,

"I believe the road to hell is paved with adverbs, and I will shout it from the rooftops. To put it another way, they're like dandelions. If you have one in your lawn, it looks pretty and unique.

If you fail to root it out, however, you find five the next day… fifty the day after that… and then, my brothers and sisters, your lawn is totally, completely, and profligately covered with dandelions.

By then you see them for the weeds they really are, but by then it's — GASP!! — too late."

Congratulations! You've just learned one of the least intuitive grammar lessons, which also means you've come to the end of this book. By now, you've learned everything you need to write grammatically and with style. By exploring one of your biggest dreams, you've explored the depths of English grammar.

The Narrative

The Dream Narrative Summarized

Throughout this book, we've used your dream as the narrative to explain English grammar. To recap, here are the main elements you need to remember about English grammar:

1. Your dream has several layers of depth which you can explore.
2. If your dream lacks a character or an action, your dream dies.
3. There is a sequence to your dream, and you must respect the sequence for your dream to occur.
4. The variables in your dream aren't equally significant.
5. Your dream must have an independent variable.
6. Most often, your dream doesn't involve just you, the subject, but also others, the objects.
7. The characters and actions of your dream are often more complicated than they appear.
8. The actions of your dream depends on the context in which they are located.
9. There is another way to think about the context in which you act out your dream.
10. A simple dream has only one independent variable.

11. A complex dream has not only an independent variable, but also a dependent variable.
12. You can compound your dream by adding independent variables.
13. You can make your dream more complex or compound it, but you can also do both.
14. You'll take pauses between the different parts of your dream.
15. Some pauses show the end of something neutrally and others with omissions.
16. Some parts of your dream will be more intense than others.
17. Some parts of your dream will leave you with questions.
18. Some parts of your dream stick together to make sense.
19. Some parts of your dream belong to another.
20. Conversations occur as part of your dream.
21. Your dream requires simple pauses.
22. Your dream requires complex pauses.
23. Some parts of your dream are introduced by a previous event.
24. Your dream gets connected and disconnected by events.
25. Your dream sometimes contains unnecessary information.
26. Your dream's style is made of its components.
27. You can't talk about your dream to everybody the exact same way.
28. You can talk about your dream in different tones.
29. You should waste no time when talking about your dream.
30. Your dream should be authentic and filled with interesting moments.

Acknowledgments

I'm grateful to many people for their support during my journey writing this book and my journey leading to this book.

For the past months, I've been blessed with the help of Aris Kalamaras in my business and for this book. He has been revising, editing, and proofreading my work diligently. I met Aris in a composition class at Concordia University, and he edited a blog post I wrote as an assignment. Ironically, this blog post turned out to be the fetus of this book. I am also grateful to Paul Spitzer, who has provided valuable feedback on this book.

My parents instilled in me a passion for reading when I was a child. They encouraged me to read and write instead of playing video games. Although I wasn't happy about their video games restrictions, I now acknowledge it has been a good thing. I can't thank them enough for the way they raised me. I am also grateful to my sister, who has always challenged me and encouraged me in my writing endeavors.

This book wouldn't exist if it weren't for two women who took a chance on me while I was in university. Juliet and Jen hired me to work as a writing assistant at Concordia University's writing center, and it has been a life-changing opportunity that set me on my career path. I wouldn't understand writing the way I do were it not for my experience as a writing assistant. I would not have founded Trivium Writing either.

I am grateful for the administrators at Green Valley College in South Koronadal, Philippines, for commissioning me to write this book and for their trust throughout this process: Dr. Romeo Sustiguer, Sr., Dr. Luz A. Sustiguer, MBA, Dr. Rj Sustiguer, Dr. Nida Pastor, Joylen Pisaro, Micheallie Carbonquillo, and Rosalie Cabeltes.

For the past year, I have been dedicating myself entirely to building my business, Trivium Writing, and I could not be more grateful to my early clients, who have made me a better writer and teacher: Aaron, Alelia, Angela, Cierra, Cindy, Cris, David, Dave, Eric, Ghulam, Jackie, Kendra, Laura, Gareth, Richard, Rebecca, Rose, Robin, Sarama, and Yasha.

I am also grateful to my early business mentors, who helped me build my business to what it is now, which put me in the position to write this book: Alex, Anthony, Chris, Dan, Josh, Matt, Rudy, Taylor, and Travis. These people expanded my notion of what's possible and truly put me on the path to becoming the best version of myself.

I am fortunate to be surrounded by caring and loving friends who push me to be the best version of myself every single day: Aaron, Ali, Bijal, Carlos, Cierra, Federica, Frank, Hamza, Scott, Leslie, Matthew, Michael, Oksana, Yves-Denis, and Zurlia.

GLOSSARY

GRAMMATICAL TERMS WITH DEFINITIONS

An overview of the 4 levels of analysis in a sentence (parts of speech, word roles, phrases, and clauses).

Writing is an organic task. With practice, it unfolds naturally, and you don't need to think about grammar to do it. However, it is still a good idea to be familiar with grammatical terms and to remember them. By being comfortable with grammar, you can more easily improve your writing. Here is a glossary of the grammatical terms discussed in this book with their definitions:

1.1 Parts of Speech (Words)

Parts of speech are different **word categories**. They are the most specific level of analysis. Most parts of speech tell us information such as **"who," "what," "where," "which," "whose," "when," "to whom," "how,"** and **"why."** Some, like determiners, conjunctions, and interjections, do not provide such information.

Words, however, **cannot always** provide information by themselves. They often need to be put together to give the information such as *"who," "what," "where," "which," "whose," "when," "to whom," "how," and "why."*

1.1.1. Determiners

Words used to clarify the noun.

- **Article**: express the **specificity or generality** of the noun.
  Ex.: a, an, the
- **Demonstratives:** point to **the noun** they replace.
  Ex.: this, that, these, those, which, etc.
- **Possessives:** indicate **to whom** an object belongs.
  Ex.: my, your, our, their, his, hers, whose, my friend's, our friends', etc.
- **Quantifiers**: indicate **the general**.
  Ex.: few, a few, many, much, each, every, some, any, etc.
- **Numbers**: indicate **the number** of people or objects.
  Ex.: one, two, three, twenty, forty
- **Cardinals**: indicate **the numeral position** of someone or something.
  Ex.: first, second, 1st 2nd, 3rd, last, next, etc.

1.1.2. Nouns

Words used to identify people, animals, plants, objects, places, etc.

- **Common nouns**: refer to people or things in general.
  Ex.: Man, woman, policeman, teenager, city, park, etc.
- **Proper nouns**: identify a particular person, place or thing.
  Ex.: Toronto, Canada, Justin Trudeau, Friday, etc.
- **Concrete nouns**: refer to objects that can be perceived by one or more of the five senses.
  Ex.: flower, music, bear, pie, tornado, colony, milk, etc.
- **Abstract nouns**: refer to intangible ideas, qualities, and conditions.
  Ex.: truth, danger, experience, compatibility, etc.
- **Collective nouns**: refer to groups of people or things.
  Ex.: audience, family, government, team, group, jury, etc.

- **Count nouns**: refer to nouns that can be counted and thus have a plural form.
  Ex. : books, shelves, tables, apples, etc.
- **Mass nouns:** refer to nouns that cannot be counted and so don't have a plural form. They are not preceded by an article (a, an, the).
  Ex.: rain, flour, earth, wine, etc.

Note that some nouns can be countable in some contexts while uncountable in others. For example, you can say, "These are the fundamental truths about human nature," in which the noun "truth" is countable. But you can also say, "There's no truth in what he said," in which the noun "truth" is uncountable.

1.1.3. Pronouns

Words that replace a given noun.

- **Personal pronouns**: represent a grammatical person.
  Ex.: he, she, they, it, etc.
- **Demonstrative pronouns**: represent nouns and their positions.
  Ex.: this, that, these, those, etc.
- **Interrogative pronouns**: help formulate questions.
  Ex.: which, who, what, where, etc.
- **Indefinite pronouns**: represent people without saying exactly who they are.
  Ex.: none, several, all, few, anything, etc.

1.1.4. Verbs

Words that describe an action or indicate the existence of something.

- **Action verbs**: express what happens in a sentence.
- **Transitive verbs**: require a direct object to make sense.
  Ex.: bring, give, order, play, etc.
- **Intransitive verbs**: do not require a direct object to make sense.

Ex.: adapt, fly, rise, shine, die, etc.

- **Linking verbs**: create a connection between the subject and information about the subject.
  Ex.: act, appear, be, feel, remain, turn, etc.
- **Helping verbs**: are placed before another verb to add detail.
  Ex.: can, may, must, shall, will, could, etc.

1.1.5. Adjectives

Words that modify a noun or a pronoun.

- **Proper adjectives**: are based on names and describe people, and things. They need to be capitalized.
  Ex.: Russian, British, Canadian, American, Shakespearian, Renaissance, etc.
- **Descriptive, qualitative or attributive adjectives**: express the nature of the person or object discussed.
  Ex.: adaptable, brave, blue, dangerous, old, young, etc.
- **Quantitative adjectives**: express the number of the object discussed.
- **Numeral adjectives**: tells us about how many or how much or in what order the noun is.
- **Definite numerals**: give a specific idea of the number of nouns
- **Cardinals**: regular numbers.
  Ex.: one, two, three, four, five, six, etc.
- **Ordinals**: tell us the position of a noun.
  Ex.: first, second, third, fourth, fifth, etc.
- **Multiplicatives**: tell us how many time to multiple.
  Ex.: single, double, tripe, quadruple, etc.
- **Indefinite numerals**: give a vague idea of the number of nouns.
  Ex.: Few, all, many, several, etc.

Note that if you are listing several adjectives, you must respect the following order:

- Quantity or number
- Quality or opinion
- Size
- Age
- Shape
- Color
- Proper adjective (often nationality, other place of **origin**, or material)
- Purpose or qualifier

1.1.6. Adverbs

Word that modifies, a verb, and adjective, or another adverb.

- **Adverbs of time**: help express the WHEN.
  Ex.: already, today, tomorrow, now, then, yet, already, etc.
- **Adverbs of manner**: help express the HOW.
  Ex.: accidentally, badly, cruelly, kindly, poorly, etc.
- **Adverbs of degree**: help express the HOW.
  Ex.: almost, barely, extremely, just, nearly, very, deeply, etc.
- **Adverbs of place**: help express the WHERE.
  Ex.: above, abroad, back, behind, downstairs, here, etc.
- **Adverbs of frequency**: help express the HOW OFTEN.
  Ex.: always, constantly, daily, sometimes, etc.

1.1.7. Prepositions

Words used to show the relationship between words, phrases, or clauses.

- **Prepositions of time**: help express the WHEN.
  Ex.: at (noon, midnight), in (April, the summer), on (Tuesday, Christmas day), etc.
- **Prepositions of place**: help express the WHERE.
  Ex.: at (my house, the restaurant), in (the city), on (the table), etc.

- **Prepositions of direction or movement**: help express the WHERE.
  Ex.: towards (the bus stop), to (the shop), through (the glass), into (the ground), to, from, under, along, etc.
- **Prepositions of agent**: help express the WHAT.
  Ex.: by (the judge), with (a pen), etc.
- **Prepositions of instrument**: help express the HOW.
  Ex.: by (plane), with (your key), on (my laptop), etc.

1.1.8. Conjunctions

Words used to link clauses, phrases, or words.

- **Coordinating conjunctions**: join words, phrases, and clauses together that are grammatically equal.
  Ex.: for, and, nor, but, or, yet, so (FANBOYS)
- **Subordinating conjunction**: introduce dependent clauses in a sentence and describe the relationship between clauses.
  Ex.: after, although, as far as, in that, once, since, supposing that, unless, when, etc.
- **Correlative conjunctions**: join equal sentence elements to describe their relationship.
  Ex.: either… or; neither… nor; both… and; not only… but also.

1.1.9. Interjections

Words used a single utterance to show an emotion.

- **Interjections for greetings**: express salutations.
  Ex.: hi, hello, hey, etc.
- **Interjections for joy**: express a feeling of joy.
  Ex.: yay, hourra, etc.
- **Interjections for approval and praise**: express a positive feeling.
  Ex.: bravo, congrats, etc.

- **Interjections for surprise**: express a feeling a surprise.
  Ex.: gosh, dang, etc.
- **Interjections for grief/pain**: express a feeling of grief or pain.
  Ex.: ouch, ah, alas, etc.
- **Interjections for bidding farewell**: express farewells.
  Ex.: bye, goodbye, farewell, etc.
- **Interjections for expressing doubt or hesitation:** show doubt or hesitation.
  Ex.: hmm, uh, er, etc.

1.2. Word Roles (Words)

Words don't always play the same role in a sentence, so parts of speech are limited in the way they describe words. Word roles don't say what words are, but rather what words do. Note that certain words roles bear the same names as parts of speech, which may cause confusion.

1.2.1. Subject

The person or object completing the action in the sentence.

- **Part of speech**: noun (and other parts of speech needed for a noun phrase).
  Ex.: "John" in "John takes the ticket."

1.2.2. Verb

The action that indicates what happens in the sentence.

- **Part of speech**: verb (and other parts of speech needed for a verb phrase)
  Ex.: "Takes" in "John takes the ticket."

1.2.3. Direct Object (DO)

The receiver of the verb.

- **Part of speech**: noun (and other parts of speech needed for a noun phrase)

  Ex.: "the ticket" in "John takes the ticket."

1.2.4. Indirect Object (IO)

The receiver of the direct object.

- **Part of speech**: noun (and other parts of speech needed for a noun phrase)

  Ex.: "to me" in "John gives the ticket to me."

1.2.5. Adverb

The modifier to a verb, an adjective, or another adverb.

- **Part of speech**: adverb (and other parts of speech needed for an adverbial phrase)

  Ex.: "slowly" in "John slowly gives the ticket to me."

1.2.6. Preposition

The indicator of relationship between different words.

- **Part of speech**: preposition

  Ex.: "to" in "John slowly gives the ticket to me."

1.2.7. Object of preposition (OP)

The object whose relationship is indicated by the object of preposition.

- **Part of speech:** noun (and other parts of speech needed for a noun phrase)

  Ex.: "me" in "John slowly gives the ticket to me."

1.2.8. Possessive

Adding an apostrophe (') and an (s) to a word to indicate that the following word belongs to it.

- **Part of speech**: noun, pronoun
- With pronouns, we use the possessive pronouns: mine, yours, his/hers, theirs, ours, their.

1.3. Phrases (Groups of Words)

Phrases are groups of words that convey information such as "who," "what," "where," "which," "whose," "when," "to whom," "how," and "why." When words (parts of speech) cannot provide the information, the phrase can. Sentences are made of multiple phrases that provide the necessary information to provide readers with meaning.

1.3.1. Noun phrase

Small part of a sentence that acts as a noun.

Ex.: "the penthouse," "the beautiful penthouse," or "the extremely beautiful penthouse."

1.3.2. Verbal phrase

Small part of a sentence that acts as a verb.

Ex.: "is searching," "can go," "could have done," "must see," etc.

1.3.3. Adjective phrase

Small part of a sentence that acts as an adjective.

Ex.: "overly enthusiastic," "very small," "who seems upset," etc.

1.3.4. Adverbial phrase

Small part of a sentence that acts as an adverb.

Ex.: "right here," "right here by the garage," etc.

1.3.5. Prepositional phrase

Small part of a sentence that acts as a preposition.

Ex.: "with the black hat," "on the table," "by my car," "toward my place," etc.

1.3.6. Conjunctional phrase

Small part of a sentence that acts as a conjunction.

Ex.: "as soon as," "as quickly as," "neither you nor I," etc.

1.4. Clauses (simple ideas)

Clauses are simple ideas, made of multiple phrases, that provide more than one piece of information such as "who," "what," "where," "which," "whose," "when," "to whom," "how," and "why."

1.4.1. Independent clauses

Part of a sentence that can stand on its own.

Ex.: Léandre bought the penthouse.

1.4.2. Dependent clauses

Part of a sentence that cannot stand on its own.

Ex.: Because bought the penthouse.

1.4.3. Defining relative clauses

Part of a sentence that adds necessary information.

Ex.: The policemen ***who face charges*** *need to find an attorney.*

Without the defining relative clause, the sentence would not make sense. We would wonder which policemen are we talking about?

1.4.4. Non-Defining relative clauses

Part of a sentence that adds non-necessary information.

Ex.: The policemen, ***who arrested a teenager today,*** *came home to his wife.*

Without the non-defining relative clause, the sentence still makes sense. It is simply not as precise.

1.5. Sentences (Complex Ideas)

Sentences are complex ideas, made of one or multiple clauses, that provide more than one piece of information such as "who," "what," "where," "which," "whose," "when," "to whom," "how," and "why.

1.5.1 Simple sentence

Sentence that comprises only one independent clause.

Ex.: Léandre bought the penthouse.

1.5.2. Complex sentence

Sentence that comprises one independent clause and one dependent clause.

Ex.: Before going out, Léandre bought the penthouse.

1.5.3. Compound sentence

Sentence that comprises more than one independent clause.

Ex.: Léandre bought the penthouse, and he took out a loan.

1.5.4. Compound-Complex sentence

Sentence that comprises more than one independent clause and at least one dependent clause.

Ex.: Before going out, Léandre bought the penthouse, and he took out a loan.

Abbreviations Used in the Book

- Def. Art. Definite article
- Adj. Adjective
- Def. Art. Definite Article
- Ind. Art. Indefinite Article
- Pr. Pronoun
- Prep. Preposition
- D.A. Definite article
- I.A. Indefinite Article

Next Steps

Where to Get More Information, Resources, and Content

Did you get to the end of this book and want to learn more about writing? To learn more about Trivium Writing's products, services, and resources, visit:

- **Website**: triviumwriting.com
- **Facebook**: facebook.com/triviumwriting
- **Instagram:** www.instagram.com/triviumwriting
- **LinkedIn**: linkedin.com/company/triviumwriting
- **Twitter**: twitter.com/triviumwriting

To learn more about Léandre Larouche and stay up-to-date with his work, visit:

- **Website:** leandrelarouche.com
- **Facebook:** facebook.com/leandrelarouche
- **Instagram:** instagram.com/leandre_larouche
- **LinkedIn:** linkedin.com/in/leandre-larouche
- **Twitter:** twitter.com/leandrelarouche

Manufactured by Amazon.ca
Bolton, ON

29023366R00160